Advance Pra
Parenting for a E

"This book is a map to the world I wa... .. ..ss .. thought and intensely practical suggestions, these authors meet the overwhelm of the current epoch with spiritual practices to experience delight, hope, and joy through cultivating values like kindness, justice, and ecological care in the lives of children. These ingredients for the world we want to inhabit do not come about by accident. If you're in need of inspiration and support to soulfully nurture the children in your life, allow this cadre of authors to become your companionship circle on the journey. They understand that the private and personal is always political. What we do in our homes affects how we engage in the public square. How we shape the lives of children, shapes the whole world. You do not need to have kids of your own to appreciate the beauty and brilliance of this book. It a gift to all who care about children and the world. Adults will find this book equally enriching for our own spiritual lives! I can't recommend it highly enough."
— Cody J. Sanders, American Baptist Chaplain to Harvard University
    and author of *A Brief Guide to Ministry with LGBTQIA Youth*

"What a lovely, fantastic, deeply moving book! It speaks to a real need among people of faith: how to tackle the seemingly opposing and impossible tasks of parenting well *and* working toward justice. Overflowing with concrete, practical, constructive suggestions and beautifully and accessibly written, this is a book you'll want to pass on to family, friends, and congregation."
— Dr. Bonnie J. Miller-McLemore, Professor, The Divinity School
    and Graduate Department of Religion, Vanderbilt University and
    author of *In the Midst of Chaos: Care of Children as Spiritual Practice*

"This book addresses difficult questions that parents often face. Do I preserve childhood innocence or expose children to realities of suffering and injustice? How can parents and children, who are already burdened with hectic schedules, be responsive to the plight of others locally and worldwide? Each chapter inspires readers to envision and enact opportunities for transformative parenting."
— Luther E. Smith, Jr., PhD, Professor Emeritus of Church and
    Community, Emory University

"A deep well of creative resources for sharing faith and hope for a better world with our children. The diverse set of contributors from different racial and ethnic backgrounds, from Canada, the UK and the US, all bring a unifying vision of possibility: we can help our children build a better world—and be transformed in the process. Practical take-home activities end each chapter, and wisdom from parents of grown children joins the voices of new parents to help readers imagine faithful ways of parenting for a more just world. A blessing to read!"
— Carolyn Helsel, Ph.D., author of *Anxious to Talk about It: Helping White People Talk Faithfully about Racism.*

"Through all my high-minded preaching, teaching, and writing on social justice and environmental care, it's been the raising of two daughters that has challenged me most acutely with the question: can I actually live this stuff out? Balancing budget, ethics and time are all hard, let alone your children's desire to fit in with their peers, with all the demands that brings. *Parenting for a Better World* welcomes you into a community of parents also wrestling with those challenges. You›ll sympathise, learn, laugh, maybe cry, and definitely be inspired and motivated to do family life together in a way that takes care of God's wonderful world."
— Dr Ruth Valerio, author of *Planet Protectors: 52 Ways to Look After God's World* and Global Advocacy and Influencing Director at Tearfund.

"*Parenting for a Better World* not only provides rich, faith-filled ideas for Christian parents and children, the essays transform into a community of support. I could feel the care, understanding, and encouragement bursting off the page from each author, giving me the confidence to try something new. Parents, Christian educators, and pastors will find in these essays creative ways to nourish the justice seeking synapses of future generations and reshape what intergenerational faith living looks like in our current times."
— Kate Ott, author of *Sex + Faith: Talking with Your Child from Birth to Adolescence*

• • • • •

This book made possible, in part, by a gift from Mike and Laura Hatler in honor of the Children, Youth, and Families of the Central Rocky Mountain Region of the Christian Church (Disciples of Christ).

• • • • •

For our families

SOCIAL JUSTICE PRACTICES FOR
YOUR FAMILY AND THE PLANET

Parenting for a Better World

Edited by
Susanna Snyder & Ellen Ott Marshall

chalice
press

Saint Louis, Missouri

An imprint of Christian Board of Publication

ChalicePress.com

Print: 9780827231863

EPUB: 9780827231870

EPDF: 9780827231887

Printed in the United States of America

Contents

Acknowledgments

This book emerged from a conversation between two friends during the pandemic—one in the US and one in the UK—both of us grappling with how to be a good parent while at the same time working toward social and ecological justice in the world. We reached out to other friends and colleagues who graciously joined the project as contributors. Together, we produced this book for all children everywhere, including our own: Linus, Elia, Jared, Noah, Hannah, Adam, Caleb, Agnes, Isaiah, Keir, Bethany, Martha, Maya, Cruz, Adrian, Solveig, Lars, Eli, Jairo, Evan, Desmond, Jennifer, Emily, Elizabeth, Carrie, Katherine, Steve, and Zoe.

Parenting for a better world is not accomplished only by parents. We are grateful to our families, friends, parishioners, students, and colleagues for shaping the work and supporting the book.

We would also like to thank Ulrike Guthrie for her careful editing, and Jennifer Carlier for her research assistance and good will with every random task. Thanks also to Chalice Press for helping us to turn the conversation among friends into this book, which we hope contributes to fruitful activities and reflection among other friends and families for years to come.

Introduction—"It's Just Too Hard"

Susanna Snyder and Ellen Ott Marshall

Parenting is hard. Working for social and ecological justice is hard. So how on earth are we to do both? We posed this question to thirteen very different parents who—like you—share a commitment to make the world a better place. You probably don't need a book to tell you that trying to parent *and* to strive for justice in the world feels overwhelming. You barely even have time to read a book like that. But maybe you'd welcome a reminder that you are not alone in your commitments and concerns. Maybe you're looking for some new ideas about what, when, and how to act. Maybe you're wanting to reflect on how any or all of this connects with your faith. Each chapter in this book explores a challenge our world faces, suggests ways in which we might respond to it as parents, and thinks about where God might be in it all. Each is written with honesty, and by parents who come from a range of backgrounds and contexts. Together, we invite you to try out practices that we have found to be practical, meaningful, and even joyful. We hope that you will find in and through us both companions on your journey and insight into experiences that differ from your own.

Struggling and Juggling

To say that there is much to be done to make the world a better place is to state the obvious. Racism, sexism, homophobia, ableism, militarism, and violence of all kinds are endemic, and that is not even to mention the huge challenge of climate change—a reality that is already destroying habitats, homes, and livelihoods and that threatens the very future of life on this planet. These issues are so big and so intertwined that it can feel impossible to know what we can do to make a difference. Meanwhile, parenting is a full-time job that requires full-on investment. At different ages and stages, parents

1

may need to grapple with newborn night waking and toddler temper tantrums, support a child struggling to learn or make friends at school, and ferry children around and help them navigate social media and mental health issues. Many of us also have to worry daily about how to raise our children to be resilient and safe in the face of endemic systemic racism and police brutality or anti-LGBTQI+ bullying. And all of this is in addition to the daily grind of preparing meals, doing never-ending laundry, and tidying up. Many of us juggle parenting with other demanding responsibilities too, paid employment and membership of a church among them. Contemporary life is full of pressure for us to achieve, own, do, be more and better, and to help our children do all that too. In sum, making a difference in the world and parenting can feel like competing priorities.

No wonder it is easy to feel overwhelmed! In response, we either throw our hands up in despair and try to numb ourselves and ignore what is going on (perhaps through drinking too much alcohol, buying more, or throwing our entire energy into being the most amazing parents we can be). Or we embark on frenzied action, doing everything we can all the time—flitting around from one cause to another, burning ourselves out and losing the joy in life.

What if we told you that there are many ways to integrate parenting, work, social justice, and creation care in your everyday life—ways that require intentionality but don't have to leave you exhausted or feeling pulled in different directions?

Sharing Diverse Stories and Practices

Through this book, we are inviting you to enter into a community of parents who are wanting to be and act in ways that make the world a better place. Each author offers one answer to the question: How can we parent in this world as people of Christian faith committed to social and ecological transformation? We suggest that meditation, growing vegetables, making collages, singing, giving, eating together, praying, waiting on others, being angry, listening, cultivating kindness along with intimacy and solidarity, joining street protests, and engaging in community organizing can all contribute to social justice and the flourishing of the earth—and can all be done while parenting. We weave together our own stories of caregiving and activism with scripture and theology, hoping that this will affirm your sense of calling in all its beauty and challenge and remind you that God is present in the middle of it all.

The ways in which we each parent for a better world need to reflect the particular nature of our own household with its distinctive concerns, gifts, and capacities. We authors are diverse, with different national, social, racial, cultural, and family backgrounds (nuclear, extended, and adoptive; with heterosexual or LGBTQI+ parents) as well as varied caregiving and vocational contexts. We hope that you will be able to find yourself in the book—that you will find yourself resonating with voices that echo or spark connections with your own experience—along with being enriched by entering into the experiences of those whose lives are very different to yours. We authors all live in the US, Canada, or the UK. As Western nations, we share much in common, including colonial pasts (and presents), increasing political division and the rise of far right politics, as well as neo-liberal, consumerist capitalist economies. Churches in these three countries are also following similar trajectories and facing similar challenges, including decline and financial instability, aging congregations, splits between those who identify as evangelical and progressive, as well as ecclesial histories and practices of colonialism, racism, sexism, and other forms of exclusion. So, while our contexts inevitably differ in many ways, there is much that we can learn from one another.

As authors, we all recognise ourselves to be on a journey where we make mistakes, revise our plans, try again, and discover new strategies. We are not claiming to have got it right, to have the answers. For each of us, the practice that we outline is just one of the ways in which we engage with injustice, and this does not mean that this practice will work for you or that this practice on its own is enough. We're not presenting a blueprint for action. Rather, we are sharing some ideas that have emerged through our own struggles. Parenting for a better world has got to be about the piecemeal and the "good-enough" as well as about high ideals and courage. Fortunately, as Brené Brown reminds us, "incredibly imperfect moments" can be "the most powerful meaning moments in our relationships with our children."[1]

---

[1]Brené Brown, *The Gifts of Imperfect Parenting: Raising Children with Courage, Compassion and Connection* (Louisville, CO: Sounds True, 2013), audiobook.

So, choose what fits your experience, identity, and context! Improve on these ideas and add to them! Be brave and gentle with yourself at the same time, embrace the good enough, and affirm the small, imperfect attempt.

The Everyday Is Important

A few key insights permeate the chapters in this book. One is that the everyday is crucially important. While we often think about social or ecological activism as being about big one-off events, what we do on an everyday basis—what is woven into the fabric of our mundane, daily lives—is critical to the unfolding of ecological and social justice. Certainly some of the chapters discuss an important, dramatic moment. But you will discover that much of our focus is on the routine and small. Pragmatically speaking, for parents, social justice work often has to be woven into our domestic lives or it simply won't happen. More deeply, we are formed as people through the everyday: Our routine practices shape us and help us to become the kind of people who know how to act for good when the big moments appear. Most of how we affect the world takes place in the actions that we take hour by hour—in what we buy, with how we spend our time, and to whom we relate and how. So, to be a caring, fully present parent does not mean shelving our justice work until we have time again. Rather, it requires us to find small ways to live out our vocation for justice and nourish a passion for justice *as* a parent, *with* our kids. The concerns and the people to whom our kids see us giving our time and energy on a regular basis shape what they in turn consider to be important and meaningful.

The Private Is Political

Related to this, all too often the home is seen as private—a space entirely separate from the machinations of the world beyond the front door. What happens in one's own home is frequently regarded as one's own business, something that has little connection with politics, economics, society, and the environment. The authors in this book see things differently. We believe that the private or personal is always political. The individual and familial is always communal and societal. This means that what we say and do at home—what we eat, how we choose to spend our time, what we watch on TV, how we bring up our children—are all intrinsically and inescapably political acts.

Deep Work and Emotional Labor

Parenting for global justice isn't only—or even mostly—about particular actions that you do or don't take, individually or as a family. It is not primarily about time management and priority setting (although that can help). More profoundly, parenting for global justice involves tremendous emotional labor and demands a willingness to engage in the internal work of reflection, integration, affirmation (of self and others), and letting go. It requires courage. Parents who are honest with themselves and their kids need to learn to work constructively with anger, fear, discouragement, self-doubt, and overwhelm. From a variety of caregiving contexts, this book expresses strong emotions, offers solidarity to parents who feel them, and provides strategies for helping families work through them together. We share our own struggles of grappling with how our parenting practices contribute to justice, and the ways that our justice work informs our parenting. Theologian Wendy Farley offers a helpful reminder: "To love children and, through them, to love the world is not sentimental piety; it is warrior energy and requires enormous courage."[2]

Spiritual Practice, Encountering God, and Growing in Faith

Spiritual practices thread their way throughout the chapters. We offer a variety of suggestions for how you can connect parenting for a better world with your faith. We describe practices such as cultivating kindness, listening, singing lullabies, and praying as justice-fostering spiritual practices that you can do with your kids. We also provide examples of spiritual reflection using scripture, journaling, and the arts. We offer explorations of biblical stories as well as theological ideas to help you think and pray through what you want to do, either individually or with others in a study group. We do this because our spiritual lives provide a crucial foundation—the water table into which we sink our roots—to sustain this hard work. What is more, we encourage you to see justice practices as spiritual practices themselves. So, you will find in this book an invitation *both* to integrate spiritual practices into your family life and activism *and* to understand family life and activism as spaces in which we encounter the sacred

---

[2]Wendy Farley, "Courage Unparalleled Opened Her Utterly": A Practical Theodicy," in *Parenting as Spiritual Practice and Source for Theology: Mothering Matters,* eds. Claire Bischoff, Elizabeth O'Donnell Gandolfo and Annie Hardison-Moody (London: Palgrave Macmillan, 2017), 280.

and deepen our relationship with God. Holding together parenting and working for justice is imbued with—pregnant with—possibility, opportunity, and gift. As the authors of this book attest, as well as requiring dedication and determination in the face of challenge, parenting for a better world provides endlessly fertile ground for delight, hope, and joy.

How to Use This Book

This book is, above all, an invitation to converse with us. So, use it in whatever way works best for you. You could read through it individually, chapter by chapter, or perhaps use it as the basis of discussion in a church or parenting group, reading a chapter a week or month and reflecting on how it relates to your shared and divergent experiences.

You might want to take some time to have a go at the practices suggested in the "Try It Out" section of each chapter before moving on to the next one—trying practices out one by one for a while rather than attempting all of them at once. You don't have to adopt any particular practice if you don't like it or it doesn't work for your family, but the best way to see what *is* going to work for you is actually to give it a go.

You might want to find some companions with whom to try practices, for solidarity and to compare notes afterward.

Finally, you might want to consider taking some time to be still—to pray—before you read a chapter, inviting God to be present as you explore what it means to parent for a better world.

1

Cultivating Kindness

Chine McDonald

When I became a parent, the world immediately felt different. The moment I held my baby boy in my hands, overwhelming feelings of love suddenly collided with the unwelcome realization that the world was a scary place. In that moment of clarity, I could see the world's unkindness and brokenness—a brokenness and unkindness that resulted in injustice, pain, hatred, and their outworkings of racism, sexism, homophobia, ableism, violence, and climate injustice. My long-held hope in a God of justice who made all things new took on new resonance. I desperately wanted God to be good so that my son could exist in a planet marked with goodness; a place of hope rather than despair, love rather than hatred—in short, a place of kindness.

In our antenatal classes run by the (British) National Childbirth Trust, in which we joined seven other bewildered couples who were also about to become parents for the first time, we were tasked with a range of different activities designed to prepare us for parenthood. We put nappies/diapers on dolls, took notes on the various stages of labour, and learned about breastfeeding and burping and the role that the partners in the room were expected to play in all of this.

At times it felt overwhelming, and we wondered what we had gotten ourselves into. But there was one moment that was particularly wonderful. Our instructor handed each couple a blank paper gift tag and asked us to hold it and take a moment to think together about what we hoped our baby would be like. My husband, Mark, and I wrote down three words. We hoped our son would be *fun, inquisitive,* but most of all, *kind.*

We've been parents for a few years now, and I've come to realise that this kindness does not just happen. In order to become kind, toddlers need to witness kindness, be in a community of kindness, and be creative with kindness. Being able to show kindness begins with experiencing kindness themselves and being kind to themselves. Only after that can they show kindness to others and kindness to creation.

In this chapter, I encourage you to spend time cultivating kindness in your children. This seemingly simple virtue can transform their relationship with themselves and others, and prepare the ground for them to do good in the world. A toddler who witnesses kindness at home, who is kind to themselves, to others, and to the planet, will grow up to be an adult whose heart bends toward others, who feels the pain of injustice, inequality, and unfairness, and who wants to do something about it. As Christians, the biblical witness forms us and teaches us how to cultivate such kindness.

Thinking Theologically about Kindness

The Bible mentions Tabitha, one of the early followers of Jesus, just once—in Acts 9:36–43. From the Bible account, we do not know her circumstances—whether she was rich or poor, whether she had children, whether she was single, widowed, or married. But we do know that she was kind. The only description we have of Tabitha (or Dorcas, as her name was translated in Greek) is that "she was devoted to good works and acts of charity" (v. 36). This compassion made her a beloved member of the community of faith. When she died, the members of this community were so distraught that they sent for Peter. While he was with them, he saw how sad people were that she had passed, and he was shown the fruits of her kindness and compassion to her community in the form of the garments and robes she had sewn for people. The miraculous story of Tabitha's being raised from the dead is what is typically remembered about this story. But notice also how much of a difference her kindness made to those around her. For the writer of Acts, this clearly mattered. Kindness and compassion for our communities is a symbol of a relationship with Christ, the living God, the One who calls us not merely to worship but to manifest our faith through our impact on our world.

Kindness is not just nice to have; it is a quality crucial for us to nurture because it is a foundational biblical principle that demonstrates what it is to be a human being in relationship with God. The cosmic story at the heart of the Christian faith tells a story of the ultimate kindness—that of God's love for us in the form of the Word, Jesus Christ. The Bible often describes the hope afforded humanity through the incarnation, death, and resurrection of Jesus as God's gift to all, offered freely, with no strings attached and with nothing sought in return. "Be kind to one another," we read in Ephesians 4:32.

But Christian kindness is about more than merely being nice; it brings with it a sense of altruism, of kindness without any regard for what we might get in return.

I have long been fascinated with the ideas around kindness, altruism, and the concept of selfless, sacrificial, no-strings-attached deeds of goodness. I occasionally wonder how different our world could be if each of us in our own lives acted not out of self-interest but valued others above ourselves and looked to the interests of others, as we read in Philippians 2:3–4. As fundamentally self-interested people, it is hard for us to imagine how it can be possible to offer kindness to others without the prospect of getting something back—that something including that warm, fuzzy feeling we get when we are kind to others. Theologians and philosophers have argued for centuries about whether such altruism is possible and what criteria constitute an action as a truly free gift. They suggest it includes no warm, fuzzy feeling, and no expectation of reciprocation, even if that reciprocation might be at a later date. Yet French sociologist Marcel Mauss, in his 1923 work *The Gift,* argues that giving always requires reciprocal exchange and that it can never be truly selfless.[3] There are unwritten rules about what the benefactor requires from the recipient, he says. Though it may seem impossible, the concept of individual self-interest goes against the open-hearted, selfless, and generous imperatives of the New Testament. God calls us into radical generosity, a goodness and countercultural kindness. Kindness is love in action.

---

[3]Marcel Mauss, *The Gift* (London: Routledge, 2002), 25.

But the countercultural kindness to which God calls us does not have to be shown only in grand or even cosmic gestures. For families, kindness can be demonstrated in the littlest of things, but I think it must start with being kind to ourselves.

Being Kind to Ourselves

Recalling that paper gift tag on which we wrote our hopes and dreams for our son, and recalling the realities of nurturing and cultivating kindness in someone so young, I break down such countercultural kindness into being kind to oneself, being kind to other people, and being kind to creation.

First, we must be kind to ourselves. Before we can follow the second commandment (in Matthew's gospel) to love our neighbour as we love ourselves, we first love ourselves.

It was my son who first prompted me to recognize that need to nurture kindness of self when I realised that history was repeating itself. Back when I was five years old, an immigrant child who mere months before had travelled with my family from our home in Nigeria to start a new life in the UK, I was one of only a handful of non-white children in my school in Greenwich, southeast London. One day, our teacher asked us to draw self-portraits. I vividly remember taking a light blue pencil and colouring in my eyes, then taking a pink pencil and drawing some rosy cheeks, then taking a yellow pencil and drawing my long, straight, blonde hair. I sat back and admired my creation. My friend looked over at my drawing and declared, "That's not you!" In that moment I had my first realisation of what I looked like. Instead of looking like the white girls in my class, or the Disney princesses I had seen on screen, I was brown, with black hair and dark eyes. I remember a profound sense of disappointment and shame. In that moment, rather than rejoicing in the person that God had made me to be, I was deeply disappointed in and unkind to myself.

Fast forward thirty years when I witnessed that same sense of disappointment in my little boy. At the age of two, he became fascinated with the colours of things. "What colour is the sky?" we would ask. "Blue," he'd reply. "What colour is the grass?" "Green." "What colour is Daddy?" I asked one day. And he looked up at his dad and replied, "Pink." "And what colour is mummy?" He examined my face, squinting, and said, "Brown." "And what colour are you?" He paused, looked from his mother to his father and then at himself, with an evident sense of disappointment so familiar to me, and replied, "Grey." In that moment, my husband and I—our hearts breaking at the thought of our son not loving the beautiful creation that he was—knew that we had to do something to change his perception of himself, to see himself as God sees him. I'll always be grateful to my husband for his response: "You're not grey, you're golden brown!" And our baby boy's eyes lit up. He was delighted in himself. Golden brown was his favourite colour thereafter.

To me that sense of golden-brownness demonstrates the divine thread of the *imago Dei* that runs through every human being. It's that special something that not only means each of us is an image bearer, carrying with us something of God, but also that each of us is connected to every other person. Being kind to ourselves means quieting the voices in our heads that give voice to the internalised oppression that many of us from minority groups have ingrained within us. Being kind to ourselves means standing tall in who God has made us to be and refusing to fall for the world's lies about who we are based solely on the colour of our skin, our gender, our class, or our sexuality. Being kind to ourselves means recognising the *imago Dei* in us and responding appropriately. Recognising that the image of God is also found in every other human being we encounter helps us to be kind to others.

Being Kind to Others

Toddlers are not known for their kindness to other people. In fact, I used to be so embarrassed when my son, in what's affectionately known as the "terrible twos," refused to share toys with other children. He became so possessive when others came for play dates that any attempt to encourage him to share and be kind to the other children resulted in tantrums. I was not prepared for his reaction. Were we raising a little monster? Had we done something wrong? Then I realised that this was a developmental phase that many children traverse. Kindness often does not come naturally. We have to cultivate and nurture it in our children until one day we are astonished at the generous, kind, and loving child we are raising.

One of the best ways I've found to cultivate kindness in my toddler is to practice kindness myself and make sure my son witnesses it as much as possible. At the start of the COVID-19 pandemic, perhaps as a way for me to exert control within an increasingly anxiety-inducing environment, I decided that although we could no longer see and meet up with our friends and families, we would work harder to foster community and nurture kindness among those nearest to us—our neighbours. So, on one of those early days, I created a flyer with a photograph of our family, a message letting my neighbours know that we were here if any of them needed anything, and an invitation to a WhatsApp group. Then I took my son and walked with him up and down our road posting these leaflets through our neighbours' doors. I was amazed at how keen people were to join the group. Soon most of our neighbours had joined. We shared stories about who we were, what we did, and what had brought us to the neighbourhood. We shared books and jigsaw puzzles and children's toys and surplus food. We encouraged one another when times were tough. We started a book club. We celebrated together in our street, once a week from our doorsteps applauding the National Health Service (NHS) in Britain. These are the memories that I hope my son will take with him into adulthood—those amazing moments that start with a step of kindness, a decision to demonstrate love to others.

We cannot show kindness in a vacuum. Kindness needs other people. So part of being able to show love is drawing people closer, or getting closer to them. Kindness needs community. That community can be found on your street, in school, in church, and in family.

Being Kind to Creation

That community also extends to the earth and to all life upon it. We parents must therefore teach our children what it means to be kind to creation, to be good stewards of the earth. Part of me fears that we are already too late when it comes to the climate catastrophe we have wrought upon the earth. And yet I hope—not in what has come before, but in what our children can do to save us all.

That hope prompted me, together with our son, to take to the streets as part of the Mothers Rise Up March—a march through London of parents with their children, protesting for the sake of the planet and our children's future. Of course, I know it will take more than some photos of a climate march he once attended to nurture in him a love of the planet and a responsibility to demonstrate kindness to it. It will take us parents being committed to caring for the planet and talking about the implications of our actions on those in (predominantly poor and sub-equatorial) countries who are already on the frontlines of the climate emergency. For our dual heritage son, it means thinking about our actual family in one of the countries most affected by climate change: Nigeria. It means understanding that our selfish actions in the UK can detrimentally affect our actual relatives. The connection to the Global South is not solely a theoretical one.

Some of these concepts can be hard for a child to understand. But there are simple actions that can help children to grasp the importance of being kind to the planet. We can get them involved in recycling, sorting plastics from paper and taking pride in making sure things are in the right place. We can encourage them to pay attention to the animals and creatures that live all around us, the birds or squirrels they encounter on a walk to nursery/day care or school, the snails and slugs in our garden or park. When my son notices these tiny creatures and crouches down to take a closer look, he is appreciating the wonder of creation. As parents we try to help him understand how we are all part of it and play a role in protecting it. It is important that we be kind to insects and animals as well as the humans in our communities near and far.

The Importance of Witnessing, Community, and Creativity

So how do I do that? In the early days of the coronavirus pandemic, as schools and nurseries/day cares shut down and the world took on a heightened sense of unfamiliarity and scariness, my husband and I were struggling to juggle heavy workloads with looking after our boy. Having been wrenched from nursery—where together with his friends he was occupied all day long with crafts and snack times—he suddenly found himself at home with distracted parents who were trying their best to come up with new toddler-based activities.

Over that time, one of the new books that we bought was our deliberate attempt to nurture kindness. We bought a book called *Be Kind* by Pat Zietlow Miller.[4] It is a beautiful book in which a young child starts to

---

[4]Pat Zietlow Miller, *Be Kind* (New York: Roaring Brook Press, 2018).

understand and practice kindness: kindness to a new friend at school, to their family, and to their community. We read that book every night for weeks in our attempt to foster a culture of kindness, and I'm sure it will have made a difference. But I realised it would take more than just a "show and tell" approach to cultivate kindness in a toddler. It would take creativity.

Over those weeks and months we were incredibly grateful for the creativity of our church, which recognised how important it was to hold our children close. As Sunday school moved to Zoom, with our little ones huddled around their iPads and laptops, volunteers from our church delivered little packs of goodness to our doorsteps full of envelopes with activities for the following few Sundays. One day, a pack arrived filled with nine weeks' worth of activities, each one focused on a different fruit of the Spirit, the nine characteristics that demonstrate a godly life: love, joy, peace, patience, kindness, goodness, gentleness, faithfulness, and self-control. Every Sunday morning over those two months the toddlers gathered via Zoom and were guided in a new activity, focused on that week's fruit of the spirit. Alongside several fruit-based activities, they learned about self-control with sweets/candy, they made badges for peace, they planted sunflowers to demonstrate patience, they made cards of kindness. Each week they watched an animation of a song with the catchiest of tunes, helping them to remember all the fruits of the spirit. "The fruit of the Spirit's not a che-wee," my son would say adorably, mispronouncing "cherry." Though the activities were designed for three- and four-year-olds, even I learned much in those weeks. I am grateful to our church and its committed Sunday school leaders for demonstrating how to cultivate virtues such as kindness in young children.

Try It Out

Now, over to you! What are the ways in which you can nurture and cultivate kindness in your own children? Starting with kindness to themselves, then kindness to others, and then showing kindness and care for our planet, here are some suggestions.

Kindness to Self

- Ask your child what their favourite thing about themselves is. Are they funny? Do they like the dimples in their cheeks? Are they proud of how high they can jump? Write down their responses alongside a self-portrait.

- Nurture a rhythm of self-care from a young age. Encourage your child to think about the things they like to do most—the things that bring them joy—and schedule a day once a quarter, or even once a month, on which they get to do all their favourite things.

Kindness to Others

- Ask your child to draw or paint a card to give to a neighbour and show them kindness.

- Bake some Kindness Cookies and put them in a box outside your home, encouraging neighbours and passers-by to take one by posting a sign saying: "Free Kindness Cookies. Help yourselves, and have a nice day!"

Kindness to the planet

- If you live near a beach or park, head over one Saturday morning and show kindness to the environment by going litter-picking with your child. Marvel at the good work you and your child have done to make it look beautiful.

- Help your child to write a letter to a newspaper urging global leaders to take action on climate change and encouraging them to remember those in poor communities in the Global South who are on the frontlines of climate catastrophe right now.

2

Edible Gardening

Susanna Snyder

Soil. It always gets stuck under my fingernails when I am out in the garden tending to the vegetables. It used to bother me later when I was working at my desk, but now I find it a helpful reminder that I am connected to—or more accurately, a part of—the earth. In this chapter, I explore edible gardening, a practice that I, with my family and other members of our local community, have adopted in the face of ecological crisis. Through sprinkling carrot seeds in furrows of soil carved with my fingers, and through connecting with others to encourage vegetable and fruit growing in our local community, I have been on a journey: Whereas I once felt overwhelmed, paralysed, and isolated by the enormity of climate change and environmental devastation, I am now discovering some joy and agency in our small-scale, good-enough, and community-focused gardening responses.

Facing Up to the Climate Crisis

While climate change and ecological crisis are not new, many of us have only recently become acutely aware of these catastrophic developments in the life of our planet. In 2018, the United Nations Intergovernmental Panel on Climate Change warned that we had only until 2030 to prevent the worst impacts of anthropogenic climate change. One million-plus species risk becoming extinct by the middle of this century; extreme weather events such as hurricanes, flooding, and wildfire are becoming more frequent; polar ice is melting; and the Gulf Stream is becoming unstable. Reduced water supplies are jeopardizing crop production; and those in the Global South—not least island nations and those where desert heat already suffocates—are bearing the brunt of the effects, exacerbating the marginalisation those people face due to their place in the global economy. There's plastic waste in the ocean, and humanity's lack of respect for the boundaries between humanity and wild creatures' space is responsible in large part for the COVID-19 pandemic that has devastated our world. We all now know these "inconvenient truths" (to quote Al Gore).

As someone who has long been committed to social justice, I confess to feeling gut-punched by my late-dawning recognition of the severity of the climate crisis and by many governments' lack of courage and willingness to make necessary radical economic and political changes to start addressing it. Greta Thunberg, Swedish climate activist, was right to challenge adult complacency when she said, "I don't want your hope. I don't want you to be hopeful. I want you to panic. I want you to feel the fear I feel every day, and then I want you to act. I want you to act as you would in a crisis. I want you to act as if our house is on fire. Because it is."[5] As a privileged white middle-class woman, the social injustices with which I have previously engaged have largely been the struggles of *others* (even if they were also about the nature of the society I inhabited). But *this* injustice directly affects me and my own children, now. Besides, *this* injustice of climate change seems so big and so out of our control that it is hard to know how to tackle it. It requires every government and corporation to transform what they do and how, as well as billions of individuals to change their daily lives drastically. It is interwoven with every other systemic injustice in our world—racism, sexism, classism, ableism, heterosexism, and more—a morass of consequences of white neoliberal economic colonial patriarchy.[6] The action of one human being starts to feel like

---

[5]Greta Thunberg, "'Our House is on Fire': Greta Thunberg, 16, urges leaders to act on climate," *The Guardian*, January 25, 2019, https://www.theguardian.com/environment/2019/jan/25/our-house-is-on-fire-greta-thunberg16-urges-leaders-to-act-on-climate.

[6]See Willie Jennings, *After Whiteness: An Education in Belonging* (Grand Rapids, MI: Eerdmans, 2020).

an invisible speck on a translucent thread of a complex, interconnected web of systemic oppression and destruction.

So, I found my heart sinking as a I repeatedly asked myself the question: How could one person—with caring responsibilities for a three-year-old daughter and a six-year-old son and a demanding job—begin to act (never mind effectively) in the face of the climate crisis?

A Scattered, Anxious, and Individual Approach

I began with a somewhat anxious and scattered response. My partner and I tried to make one change every few weeks. We switched our energy provider to one that used only renewables. We began to eat less meat and dairy, use less plastic, and buy more things secondhand. We developed a habit of talking with our children about the importance of not squishing bugs, and we take fewer flights. We have signed numerous petitions and taken part in climate change street marches, and a chunk of our monthly giving goes to organisations that plant trees and look after wildlife. At the seminary where I work, I have been a part of our institutional efforts toward obtaining a Bronze Award from the A Rocha UK Eco Church scheme.[7]

But all of this feels fragmentary and inadequate: We still use cars and planes, and we recognise the middle-class, first-world privilege of being able to afford more environmentally-friendly food, clothes, and insulation. Moreover, this approach feels limited and disconnected. While individual actions and behaviours are crucial, individualism (and its sibling consumerism) is also intrinsically part of the problem. I perched on a seesaw, lurching up and down between numbness—wallowing in hopelessness and inaction because it all seemed too much and too unsolvable (a state that is called *acedia* in the Christian tradition)—and desperate frenzied action to try and make a difference, at least in part to assuage my guilt and feel better about myself. That the Trappist monk and activist Thomas Merton calls this frenzy *violence* brought me up short:

> [T]here is a pervasive form of modern violence to which the idealist...most easily succumbs: activism and over-work...To allow oneself to be carried away by a multitude of conflicting concerns, to surrender to too many demands, to commit

---

[7]See "Welcome to Eco Church," https://ecochurch.arocha.org.uk/.

oneself to too many projects, to want to help everyone in everything is to succumb to violence. The frenzy of the activist neutralizes [their] work...It destroys the fruitfulness of [their]...work, because it kills the root of inner wisdom which makes work fruitful.[8]

My approach was a symptom of the very relentlessly anxious and production-driven world that lies at the root of our ecological crisis.

Plant Beans! Sow Lettuces! Harvest Tomatoes!

So, what do I suggest? That you grow your own fruit and vegetables, and do so in ways that encourage environmental awareness and justice as well as social justice.

I had already dabbled in growing vegetables and fruit in our garden for a few years when, in the pandemic autumn of 2020, a few different experiences and conversations came together to generate a related and broader idea. The local primary/elementary school that my son attends, along with other local community groups, organised a couple of events. The first was a scarecrow hunt. Each participating household made a scarecrow and put it outside their dwelling, then invited the community to use a map to find and admire them all. The second was a community lights festival. We created colourful windows that people could see on a walk around the neighbourhood. These were wonderful events for raising spirits and connecting us (at a physical distance) with one another.

Simultaneously, I was reading *The Well-Gardened Mind* by Sue Stuart-Smith, which explores the links between mental health and gardening.[9] One particularly captivating chapter told of a project called "Incredible Edible" in Todmorden, Yorkshire. In 2008, local people turned disused ground in their community—a town run down due to the closure of heavy industries upon which its economy had depended—into patches of life and hope. They tended small gardens of vegetables and fruit to which local people could help themselves. The project has flourished, involves many in their community, has revitalised neglected space, and has inspired people across the world. The tag line is "Creating a kind,

---

[8]Thomas Merton, *Conjectures of a Guilty Bystander* (London: Burns and Oates, 1968), 73. I've inserted [their] to make the original language used gender inclusive.

[9]Sue Stuart-Smith, *The Well-Gardened Mind: Rediscovering Nature in the Modern World* (New York: William Collins, 2020).

confident and connected community," and this is how the participants describe themselves:

> We are passionate people working together for a world where all share responsibility for the future wellbeing of our planet and ourselves.
>
> We aim to provide access to good local food for all, through
>
> - working together
> - learning—from cradle to grave
> - supporting local business
>
> All with no paid staff, no buildings, no public funding: radical community building in action.
>
> Membership: If you eat you're in.[10]

As I began talking with a few people in my own community—on the walk to and from school, while picking up compost from the local garden centre—we had an idea: to establish a small-scale food-growing and foraging project in our part of Oxford. "Edible Cutteslowe" now involves a range of community groups and organisations, from the horticultural therapy and garden project to the school and community larder/pantry (which addresses food insecurity and wastage in our neighbourhood). Each does what works best for them in relation to the broad idea. There's a vegetable and herb bed in the local park, and the school has not only created a bed with strawberries, herbs, and beans in it, but has appointed student ambassadors and distributed seed kits to be grown at home. We have held an online public talk and idea-generating session, and we are encouraging people to grow food at home—in a patch of ground or in a pot on their balcony or deck or front step—and to allow neighbours to help themselves to the produce if they wish. Members of the community larder/pantry and parents and carers were offered small courgette/zucchini plants in pots with "Edible Cutteslowe" labels to set out someplace, and we are making links with another local group that is in the process of planting a community orchard. Our tag line is "Growing Food, Growing Community."[11]

---

[10]See "Incredible Edible Todmorden," https://www.incredible-edible-todmorden.co.uk/ and "Incredible Edible Network," https://www.incredibleedible.org.uk/.

[11]See "Edible Cutteslowe," https://ediblecutteslowe.garden/.

Edible Gardening as Theological and Ethical Practice

As I reflected theologically on what we are trying to do in this project—which includes church partners but is not in any way a Christian- or faith-based initiative—it struck me that gardening, and perhaps edible gardening in particular, has deep roots in the biblical tradition.

The Bible talks about gardens and gardening in contexts of oppression and as a response to injustice. While the Garden of Eden features at the beginning of the book of Genesis (2:15), Genesis was actually written during the Babylonian exile, a time when the people of Israel experienced the trauma of being uprooted from their home and oppression under an imperial power. The Garden of Eden is an image of the future that God has promised to God's people, an image of renewal and hope for Israel following the exile (Isaiah 51:3). Canaan, the Promised Land, the Bible describes as a "land flowing with milk and honey" (Exodus 3:8). The garden somehow embodies right relationships between human beings, between human beings and God, and between human beings and nature—relationships that have been ruptured through human sin (urges to selfishness, violence, and possession) symbolised in the story through the disobedience of Adam and Eve.[12]

Other exilic texts similarly indicate that establishing and nurturing a garden and eating its produce was a means of survival, life, and affirming hope in a not yet imagined future:

> Thus says the LORD of hosts, the God of Israel, to all the exiles whom I have sent into exile from Jerusalem to Babylon: Build houses and live in them; plant gardens and eat what they produce. Take wives and have sons and daughters...seek the welfare of the city where I have sent you into exile, and pray to the LORD on its behalf, for in its welfare you will find your welfare. (Jeremiah 29:4–7)

---

[12]Dennis T. Olson, "Eden, The Garden of," in The *Oxford Companion to the Bible,* ed. Bruce M. Metzger and Michael D. Coogan (Oxford: Oxford University Press, online 2004 [1993]), https://ezproxy-prd.bodleian.ox.ac.uk:2460/view/10.1093/acref/9780195046458.001.0001/acref-9780195046458-e-0208. Dorothee Soelle suggests that human urges relating to ego, violence, and possession are false desires that lead to injustice. See Dorothee Soelle, *The Silent Cry: Mysticism and Resistance* (Minneapolis, MN: Fortress Press, 2001). In the New Testament, visions of rivers flowing and the tree of life producing fruit in Revelation 21–22 represent the promise of a healed, harmonious creation.

> I will restore the fortunes of my people Israel,
>
> and they shall rebuild the ruined cities and inhabit them;
>
> they shall plant vineyards and drink their wine,
>
> and they shall make gardens and eat their fruit. (Amos 9:14)

Domestic gardening—growing fruit and vegetables, as well as flowers—existed alongside agricultural cultivation, the main source of people's livelihood in ancient Israel.[13] People primarily grew cereal (wheat and barley), olives, and grapes, but also figs, pomegranates, dates, legumes, apricots, pistachios, and almonds. While vegetables do not seem to have been held in high regard—"Better is a dinner of vegetables where love is than a fatted ox and hatred with it" (Proverbs 15:17)— some people do seem to have enjoyed melons, leeks, onions, cucumbers, and garlic (Numbers 11:5; Isaiah 1:8), and (wealthy) people grew vegetable gardens (1 Kings 21:2).

American novelist, poet, and social activist Alice Walker has written of gardening as a practice of justice, of how her mother cultivated a garden in the face of the Jim Crow laws that, among other intrinsic human instincts and freedoms, sought to suppress the *creativity* of African Americans. As Walker writes, grandmothers and mothers were "Artists; driven to a numb and bleeding madness by the springs of creativity in them for which there was no release." She remembers how her mother engaged in gardening as a means of expressing her creativity—and her resistance: "My mother adorned with flowers whatever shabby house we were forced to live in...Whatever she planted grew as if by magic...a garden so brilliant with colors, so original in its design, so magnificent with life and creativity...[O]nly when my mother is working in her flowers [is she] radiant."[14]

As a privileged person engaging with climate change, I contribute to ecological devastation, so I do not want to claim an analogy with those who have gardened as a way of resisting their own oppression. But I wonder: Could even those of us who are privileged draw on this wisdom to regard sowing a lettuce seed, watering it, creating space for

---

[13] Oded Borowski, "Agriculture," in *The Oxford Encyclopedia of the Bible and Archaeology,* ed. Daniel M. Master. *Oxford Biblical Studies Online,* accessed October 18, 2021, http://www.oxfordbiblicalstudies.com/article/opr/t393/e3.

[14] Alice Walker, *In Search of Our Mother's Gardens* (San Diego: Harcourt Brace Jovanovich, 1983), 233, 241.

it by thinning out, and finally eating the leaves as an act of stubborn resistance in the face of the ecological emergency and the generational injustice that this creates? The cultivation of a vegetable or fruit plant protests in a small and almost imperceptible way the broken relationships that lie at the heart of all injustice. It quietly reasserts the caring, mutual, respectful, gentle, and generous relationship that should exist between us human beings and between human beings and the rest of creation of which we are a part. Perhaps this is what sixteenth-century Protestant reformer Martin Luther was getting at when he is reported to have said, "If I thought the world were going to end tomorrow, I would plant a tree today."

Gardening in this way slows us down and helps us to develop contemplative attention. By this I do not mean that I meditate for an hour a day in front of a kale plant. Contemplation is more truly about paying attention, about being fully present to whatever is in front of you, whether weeding a row of lettuce or tending to a family member or cooking a meal, and through that coming to recognise the reality that we are deeply connected to all that is around us and to the divine life imbued within everything.

We can be very good at numbing ourselves to reality and not seeing truly. We get caught up in busy-ness, financial and educational achieving, producing, consuming, owning, and winning. We fail to realise that the universe does not revolve around us. By thinking it does we have caused untold damage to our planet and to one another. By contrast, paying deep attention can help us cultivate amazement and wonder. We begin to notice what and who is around us, notice the presence and gift of God in all, notice sin, suffering, and injustice. Noticing a cabbage white caterpillar chewing a broccoli leaf or the first blade of an onion shoot piercing the soil or tomatoes swelling and ripening with the help of sun and good soil—all these can awaken us to the beauty and broken reality of our relationships with the earth and one another. Contemplative attention opens us to the divine presence, indwelling and whispering within our world and our souls, retuning our frequency to reality, to what really is—*to seeing with God's eyes*. Seeing like this decentres the ego. Jesus paid close attention to what was in front of him, often that which went unnoticed—the birds, the flowers, people whom society marginalised. In a similar way and in contrast to large-scale mono-cropping approaches to agriculture with their inherent appetite for volume, speed, and efficiency, when done contemplatively growing plants at home and in our neighbourhoods can reconnect us with our food and our eating and can gift *and* confront us with a "vivid feeling of interdependence" with others and creation.[15] This nudges us into further, deeper, and more radical action to challenge all that inhibits mutually nourishing relationship.

Edible gardening also reminds us unequivocally of our lack of control. There is nothing like a chard plant chewed through by slugs, curling leaves on an apple tree, rhubarb with blotches on, wonky cucumbers, and multi-rooted carrots with tendrils poking out all over them to put human beings—particularly white, affluent, and otherwise privileged ones—in their place. An early frost wilted the first planting in the main Edible Cutteslowe bed. All of this can help us to see that we are not and should not need to be in control, exercising power over all other life. It debunks the deeply entrenched colonial myth that we are or should be saviors or fixers of others. The soil that always gets stuck under my fingernails reminds me that I am part of the earth—just one dirty, embodied, formed-from-dust creature—and part of the whole ecosystem. It is for good reason that the name *Adam*—the person from whom all human beings are said to descend in Genesis 2—means in Hebrew "the one formed from the ground" and that the word *humus*—meaning "soil"—is the root of our words *human* and *humanity.* When our bodies decompose, the plants will feed on *us.* Not that we should therefore relinquish responsibility for caring for creation. Rather, edible gardening can help us to realise more deeply that we are one part of creation and that our care of our environment should not involve exploiting it for our own purposes. Incidentally, this has taught me much about how children grow—that while we can do much to try and create the right conditions for their growth and to nurture them tenderly, we cannot and should not control who they are becoming. We need to give them space.

Gardening in biblical times was a corporate rather than individual endeavour and designed (mostly) to meet the needs of the whole community. Grandparents, parents, and children were all involved in cultivation, and the law allowed those in need to glean from the edges of the fields (Leviticus 19:9–10). Then and now, edible gardening

---

[15]Wendy Farley, *Beguiled by Beauty: Cultivating a Life of Contemplation and Compassion* (Louisville, KY: Westminster John Knox Press, 2020), 120.

involves cultivating good relationships between human beings. Our garden project in Cutteslowe is bringing together people from diverse backgrounds, and we hope that people will feel free to "glean" or forage from others' garden beds and patio plant pots. A sense of community has grown among us—we are learning from one another—and an increasing number of people are stepping forward to volunteer.

The Value of Micro-Actions

There is a risk that we claim too much about a small informal project like this. After all, what difference does it make that I have a row of carrots or a pot of tomatoes growing from which people can help themselves? Edible gardening does not, by itself, right the world's wrongs and injustices. It is certainly not enough in terms of tackling our ecological emergency. All sorts of more radical personal, institutional, national, and international actions are urgently required. Nonetheless, as a grounding for other actions, edible gardening can be one contribution. It does *something*. And it is something that I can weave into the warp and weft of my daily life as a parent rather than having to do it as a separate activity for which I'd struggle to carve out time. The people I have met through my son's school, the conversations on the school walk, and the time spent outside with the children on the weekend are its life source. Edible gardening is perhaps one of what theologian Wendy Farley talks about as "micro-actions to be sprinkled through one's ordinary life."[16] While they alone do not change the world, these micro-actions "tie you to the lives of others" and have ripple effects.[17] Taking action in this way with others helps me to feel some agency and joy in responding to the immense challenge of climate change, and, rather than throw up my hands in despair, to inhabit the kind of hope that encourages me to do more. As Nigerian climate activist Oladosu Adenike puts it, "It does not matter what race, sex, tribe, country or age anyone is. Everyone can get involved in the fight for climate justice. What matters most is where we are going and what we want to achieve."[18]

---

[16]Ibid., 112.

[17]Ibid., 109.

[18]James Hanson, "3 young black climate activists in Africa trying to save the world," *Greenpeace*, October 28, 2019, www.greenpeace.org.uk/news/black-history-month-young-climate-activists-in-africa.

Try It Out

- Find a pot or use a patch of ground, and try planting some vegetable seeds in it to grow. Or buy some small seedlings/plants or fruit trees from a garden centre and grow them in pots and/ or a garden bed.

- As you tend the seedlings and then plants as they grow, contemplate what is in front of you and reflect on your own relationship with creation and the divine life imbued within everything and everyone.

- Could you share any of your harvest with neighbours, friends, or strangers? If you have an abundance, what local community food justice project might welcome some?

- Search for local communal gardening projects in urban or rural settings. Might you be able to volunteer, or go along to learn about growing vegetables—with or without your children in tow?

3

Singing Subversive Lullabies

Ingrid C. Arneson Rasmussen

Wherever we live in the world, many of us sing lullabies to our children. It's a common parenting practice. As night draws near, we caregivers cradle the next generation and sing to them. Our songs describe the world and a way of living in it.

In this chapter, I reflect on how we might think of everyday practices such as bedtime rituals as formational for the work of justice. Specifically, I invite readers to learn to sing Mary's Magnificat as a subversive lullaby that bids parent and child alike to imagine a new world and embody the risk required to usher it in.

Say His Name: George Floyd and Speaking Truth to Power

The night after George Floyd was murdered by police in Minneapolis, Minnesota, I got a call at home. The caller invited me to turn on the television and see what was unfolding around the Third Precinct, the issuing police precinct of the officers involved in Mr. Floyd's death. Righteous anger and tear gas filled the streets in equal measure. Fires—small at the time—dotted the scene. Protesters with cardboard signs stood face-to-face with police in riot gear. And there, on the corner of the screen, was the church that I serve as pastor.

The caller asked if the church would consider opening our doors to serve as the medic station for wounded demonstrators. Police were using flash bangs, rubber bullets, and tear gas liberally, which intensified the injuries being suffered. It was a big ask. Because of COVID-19, our church doors had been sealed shut for two months; we were taking seriously our commitment to slow the spread of the virus. But the twin pandemic of systemic racism was demanding our attention, and we were being asked to find our way into a future that we had never envisioned.

I was eight months pregnant at the time and had a two-year-old sleeping upstairs. When I hung up the phone and looked at my husband, he asked me one question: "Do you think this is a good idea?" "I am not sure," I responded, "but this is the call of the church at this moment in time." I quickly rang pastor colleagues and other church leaders, including one congregant protesting in the area who had a church key in his pocket. Twenty minutes later, the doors were flung wide— propped open with big wooden blocks—and I was in the car, clothed in a maternity clergy shirt, a face mask, running shoes, and uncertainty.

I had no idea what I was doing. None of my seminary courses, community organizing classes, or de-escalation trainings had prepared me fully for that moment. As I drove, questions flooded my brain: What if someone was hurt on our property? What if the building went up in flames? Do we have what demonstrators need? Is there someone else better suited to lead in this way? What will the congregation think? What will the neighborhood think? What will our insurance company think? What if we're stormed by police? Will there be weapons in the church building? How will we mitigate COVID? Is this illegal? Do I care if it's illegal? How much tear gas exposure is too much for pregnant women?

These questions and many others went unanswered. For several days and nights, the church tended to the wounded and despairing. After the fires died down and the smoke cleared, we then became a basic necessities distribution center for the neighborhood. We had gone from being a food-rich community to a food desert in a matter of days. Thousands of cars lined up to drop off food, water, plywood, saws, diapers/nappies, formula, soap, hand sanitizer, and other necessities that were no longer accessible to residents in the area.

I did not see my two-year-old daughter, Solveig, much in those days. One night I snuck home for bedtime. After washing off the remains of

smoke, tear gas, and COVID—still elusive in those early days—I went
into my daughter's room and traded places with my tired partner.
Solveig and I read her favorite stories. After we said goodnight to the
books, after she took a sip of water, and after her chubby little hand
had turned off the light, she curled herself around my pregnant form
and we held each other. She asked me to sing the "angel song"—
toddler shorthand for Mary's Magnificat from the gospel of Luke. In
the darkness, her little voice joined mine as we sang:

> An angel went from God to a town called Nazareth
>
> to a woman whose name was Mary.
>
> The angel said to her, "Rejoice, O highly favored,
>
> for God is with you.
>
> You shall bear a child, and his name shall be Jesus,
>
> the Chosen One of God Most High."
>
> And Mary said, "I am the servant of my God,
>
> I live to do your will."
>
> My soul proclaims your greatness, O God,
>
> and my spirit rejoices in you.
>
> You have looked with love on your servant here,
>
> and blessed me all my life through.
>
> Great and mighty are you, O Holy One,
>
> strong is your kindness evermore.
>
> How you favor the weak and lowly one,
>
> humbling the proud of heart!
>
> You have cast the mighty down from their thrones,
>
> and uplifted the humble of heart.
>
> You have filled the hungry with wondrous things,
>
> and left the wealthy no part.

Great and mighty are you, O Faithful One,

strong is your justice, strong your love,

as you promised to Sarah and Abraham,

kindness forevermore.

My soul proclaims your greatness, O God,

and my spirit rejoices in you.

You have looked with love on your servant here,

and blessed me all my life through.[19]

With tears, I put Solveig to bed, told her that I loved her, reminded her that her daddy was a saint, and closed her door.

I went downstairs to respond to media inquiries and other backlogged communications and was met with the news that President Trump had sanctioned police officers in riot gear to use tear gas on peaceful protesters in Lafayette Square in Washington, D.C. All of this was done, it appeared, so that he could walk from the White House to St. John's Church and pose for photos while holding a Bible—the same book that Solveig and I had just been "reading" upstairs.

A Subversive Lullaby

I haven't always thought of Mother Mary as an agitator—in fact, quite the opposite. The alternative story I'd known since childhood stemmed in part from our church's Christmas pageant. Many of us wanted to be Mary. There were countless shepherds and innumerable angels, but only one Mary after all. One year, my best friend landed the role. I can still remember how she looked with the pale blue cloth draped around her head and shoulders. She didn't have any lines in the play. Instead, the stage directions invited her to stand beside a bathrobe-wearing Joseph and look adoringly at the plastic baby Jesus, who lay perfectly still in the manger. It was a perfect performance.

I lived with that Mary—paragon of meekness and mildness—for many years until feminist theologians such as Elizabeth Johnson and

[19]Marty Haugen, "The Annunciation" and "The Magnificat," in *Holden Evening Prayer* text and tunes (Chicago: GIA Publications, 1990). Based on Luke 1:26–28, 30–32, 38, 46–55. Used with permission.

Rosemary Radford Ruether invited me to interrogate the image I had been handed. Rather than a helpless teenager, might Mary be an agent of change? Rather than a silent witness, could she be a prophetic visionary? Rather than a pawn in someone else's game, what if she were a mother bear hell-bent on protecting the most vulnerable? As different understandings of Mary and motherhood came into focus, it also became clear that any moments of quiet adoration would have been scattered between breastfeeding sessions, diaper/nappy changes, and the everyday demands of upending injustice.

Heard from of the mouth of this Mary, the Magnificat plays more subversive than sweet. This passage—featuring the longest speech by a woman in the New Testament—invites hearers to pay particular attention to those most threatened by misused power, including the sick, the self-giving, the hurting, and those held captive by practices of domination. Theologian Gustavo Gutierrez argues that "any exegesis [read: interpretation] is fruitless that attempts to tone down what Mary's song tells us about the preferential love of God for the lowly and the abused, and about the transformation of history that God's loving will implies."[20] This lullaby is the soundtrack of a real-time revolution.

Revolution? Then it's no surprise that at moments throughout history those who benefit from the status quo have perceived Mary's hymn as a threat. British authorities in India forbade the singing of the Magnificat at Evensong at the turn of the nineteenth century.[21] The junta in Argentina outlawed the Magnificat in the 1970s during the "Dirty War" after Las Madres de la Plaza de Mayo, demanding to know what had happened to their missing children and grandchildren during the military dictatorship, plastered the words in the public plaza as an act of resistance.[22] During the 1980s, the government in Guatemala found that Mary's articulation of God's special concern for the poor was too dangerous and banned it from public use.[23] I like to

---

[20]Elizabeth Johnson, *Truly Our Sister: A Theology of Mary in the Communion of Saints* (New York: Continuum, 2003), 269.

[21]Archbishop of Canterbury Justin Welby, sermon preached at Church of Ireland 150th Disestablishment Anniversary on November 25, 2019, https://www.archbishopofcanterbury.org/speaking-writing/sermons/archbishop-preaches-church-ireland-disestablishment-150th-anniversary.

[22]Sherrie M. Steiner and James T. Christi, *Religious Soft Diplomacy and the United Nations: Religious Engagement as Loyal Opposition* (Washington, DC: Lexington Books, 2021), 145.

[23]Johnson, *Truly Our Sister*, 269.

think that even when it was banned from the public square, people still sang it in private as an act of defiant devotion.

I wasn't trying to be radical when I started singing the Magnificat to baby Solveig at bedtime. Truth was, I tried to sing more traditional lullabies, but I could not remember all the words. Rather than devote time to brushing up on my nursery rhymes, I decided to go with what I knew. Pastoring meant that I could sing a setting of the Magnificat from *Holden Evening Prayer* with ease. Born out of sheer convenience, the ritual soon became something more: a nightly recitation of a new world that my daughter and I could share. The practice stuck. In addition to calming us as we sang, the lullaby cultivated a feeling of trust that, even in the face of injustice, God promised to be near.

The words took on new meaning after George Floyd was murdered by Minneapolis police and seventeen-year-old Darnella Frazier released a video of the scene she and her nine-year-old cousin witnessed outside Cup Foods at the corner of 38th and Chicago. The world watched as Minneapolis police pinned George Floyd to the ground for 9 minutes and 29 seconds; the world listened as Mr. Floyd cried out for breath and called out for his deceased mother. In the days that followed, an anonymous quote began circulating in Minneapolis and beyond: "All mothers were summoned when he called out for his momma."

Before the events of last summer, the Magnificat struck me as proclamation. Like a mother who looks at her teenager and says, "You'll do it because I said so," Mary doesn't mince words. She claims that God has scattered the proud, toppled the powerful, lifted up the lowly, and sent the rich away empty. The tense matters here; the work has already been done. Episcopal priest Barbara Brown Taylor notes that "prophets almost never get their verb tenses straight, because part of their gift is being able to see the world as God sees it—not divided into things that are already over and things that have not happened yet, but as an eternally unfolding mystery."[24]

After George Floyd, the Magnificat sounds more like a summons. By keeping us attentive to injustice and calling us to address it, it's as though Mary is inviting those who sing with her to join her in standing in the often-painful gap between the world as it is

---

[24]Barbara Brown Taylor, *Home by Another Way* (Cambridge, MA: Cowley, 1999), 18.

and the world as it ought to be. In Minneapolis, Darnella Frazier's high school English teacher, Marcia Howard, took a leave from the classroom to accompany the grieving community at George Floyd Square. In the area surrounding my church and the burned-out Third Precinct, people stepped into the fray and founded Longfellow Rising, a movement dedicated to co-laboring for a more equitable neighborhood. These feel like glimpses of what fourteenth-century German theologian Meister Eckhart meant when he wrote, "We are all meant to be mothers of God. What good is it to me for the Creator to give birth to his Son if I do not also give birth to him in my time and culture?"[25]

Practice Beginning

One month after the uprising began, I went to the hospital alone to give birth. My husband's heart condition meant that we needed to weigh the costs of COVID, and, though it was not what either of us dreamed of, the risks of hospital exposure were too great for him to accompany me. The same was true for likely substitutes. So, I packed a bag, and Paul and Solveig dropped me in the hospital cul-de-sac. I took my wheelie bag out of the trunk and rolled inside as Paul waved goodbye, saying, "It feels like we are at the airport, except we're not." Pandemics are surreal.

"Labor and delivery?" the security guard asked. Under different circumstances, I may have been offended, but I simply nodded, got my neon sticker, and headed for the elevators.

Check-in was slow. Turns out that, even in global pandemics, babies still want to be born when they want to be born. Eventually I found myself in a trauma room with a nurse named Bintou. When she asked if anyone else would be joining me, I wept. Bintou and many others carried me over the course of the ensuing forty-eight hours with hands and hearts sculpted by years of caring for strangers.

When Lars (nicknamed "Baby BLM" by my colleague because of his early participation in the movement) was born and laid in my arms, I wondered who he would be. Smartphone apps that notify parents of developmental milestones with uncanny accuracy almost convince

---

[25]Matthew Fox, *Meditations with Meister Eckhart* (Rochester, VT: Bear & Company, 1983), 74, 81.

us that we can know the future. But the truth is that none of us knows what our children's lives will hold. We all start singing before we know how the song will end. Parenting is an exercise in the unknown—the unknown for what will become of not only our lives and our children's lives, but also the life of the world.

This uncertainty, particularly in pandemic times, is isolating. I am easily convinced that the work of parenting for global justice is mine alone to do, which, of course, is nothing more than an exercise in futility. Singing Mary's Magnificat each night—first with Solveig and now also with Lars—reminds me that we learn to sing new songs when we are together. In contrast to the way that religious iconography often portrays her, Mary is always in the company of others—an angel, a partner, a conversant Jesus, a dear friend. When Gabriel appears and tells her that she's going to parent the savior of the world, she immediately takes off for the hill country to be with her bestie, Elizabeth. It's there, in the company of the community, that we hear her sing. Mary's Magnificat isn't a hero's song; it's a community song.

In the beginning, it was my voice that filled the darkened room at bedtime. It wasn't long after Solveig began speaking, however, that she began to sing with me. Her words were a bit jumbled: "My soul proclaims your *lateness*, O God, and my spirit rejoices in *blue*." I was tempted to correct her, but caught myself. Learning a new song is difficult. Solveig was taking a risk by singing. In her own way, she was teaching me how to begin.

Imperfect beginnings are hard, particularly for those of us who have been conditioned to play out all of the possible scenarios before taking on something new.[26] At an early age, I learned to conduct thorough cost-benefit analyses in all areas of life—from dating to education to employment to volunteerism to philanthropy. Many of the communities that raised me deemed this behavior to be prudent, shrewd, and faithful, and they rewarded me for it.

To be certain, discernment is a sacred gift. Like all good things, it also has an underbelly. Those of us with unearned privilege cite discernment as a reason to slow things down and deliberate from

---

[26]For further reading on risk as a spiritual practice, see Sharon Welch, *The Feminist Ethic of Risk: Revised Edition* (Minneapolis, MN: Fortress Press, 2000).

every angle, in order to ensure we choose the best outcome. In fact, this can be an exercise in control.[27] When my neighborhood was in flames and we were called to respond, it was discernment's shadow that said, "You'd better wait for the next church leadership meeting before you open those doors, Ingrid." Thankfully, my mama's heart and my colleagues invited me to resist calculation and simply said "Go!"

The opportunities for us to go—to begin—are plenty. Few are dramatic; most are mundane. Daily life is where we cultivate the capacity for courage. Whether it's cooking dinner without a recipe or spending an unplanned day with kids or responding to a neighbor's need or encouraging a colleague's innovation or participating in a social movement, there is no shortage of opportunities to practice beginning before we know the ending. As we take risks, we will fumble. (We'll add too much cayenne.) Forgetfulness will cause us to fall back into old habits. (We'll micromanage our kids' dreams.) Comfort will seduce us into what we have always known. (We'll hoard gifts that are meant to be shared.) Fear of failure will tempt us to stick with the status quo. (We'll perpetuate the myth that there is one right way.) Privilege will tell us to pull back. (We'll want all of our questions answered before committing to allyship.)

Does singing Mary's song help to prepare us to meet these moments? I can't prove causality, but I think so. This subversive lullaby finds a home in our bodies and beckons us toward a Magnificat world marked by deep listening, wholeheartedness, compassionate curiosity, and risk for the sake of the community. In the work of parenting and justice, Mary's lullaby allows us—anytime and anywhere—to rest our head on the chest of God and pay attention to the new world that is waiting to be born.

---

[27]Author Resmaa Menakem says that "white-body supremacy influences or determines many of the decisions we make, the options we select, the choices open to us, and *how* we make those decisions and choices. This operating system affects all of us, regardless of the hue of our skin....Relatively few white Americans consciously recognize, let alone embrace this subtle variety of white-body supremacy. In fact, there is often no way to measure or recognize it." Resmaa Menakem, *My Grandmother's Hands: Racialized Trauma and the Pathway to Mending Our Hearts and Our Bodies* (Las Vegas: Central Recovery Press, 2016), xix–xx.

Try It Out

- Word by word, learn to sing the Magnificat.

- Identify a moment in the day when you can weave this subversive song into your parenting (e.g., bedtime ritual, table prayer, commute to school).

- If your children have "graduated" from lullabies, you might consider learning this prayer, which is attributed to Eric Milner-White, a British Anglican priest, who served as Dean at King's College, Cambridge and Dean of York in the Church of England:

Gracious God,

you have called your people

to ventures of which we cannot see the ending,

by paths as yet untrodden,

through perils unknown.

Give us faith to go out with good courage,

not knowing where we go,

but only that your hand is leading us

and your love supporting us;

through Jesus Christ.

Amen.[28]

---

[28]"Prayer of Good Courage," *Evangelical Lutheran Book of Worship*, 317. Adapted using expansive language.

4

Praying

HyeRan Kim-Cragg

Our family cottage on Muldrew Lake near Gravenhurst, Ontario is part of a tradition. Many of the first cottagers on the lake were Christian clergy, and they built an outdoor pulpit and pews looking out at the lake from under the pine and the maple trees. This outdoor church called "Memorial Pines" is where for more than one hundred years people have held outdoor worship services in the summer.

One Sunday a few years ago my daughter, Hannah, my son, Noah, and I were sitting together at a service at the Memorial Pines when it came time to say the Lord's Prayer. Their dad (David) was leading the service. As we recited it, I noticed that both Noah and Hannah were reciting it very well. He was eleven and she was nine. Then it dawned on me that my partner David and I had never directly taught them the Prayer. Later, I asked them, "Where did you learn the Prayer?" They said, "At the church." Of course, where else? They are preachers' kids, after all.

> Our Father who art in heaven,
>
> hallowed be thy name.
>
> Thy kingdom come.
>
> Thy will be done,
>
> on earth as it is in heaven.
>
> Give us this day our daily bread.
>
> And forgive us our trespasses,

as we forgive those who trespass against us.

And lead us not into temptation,

but deliver us from evil.

For thine is the kingdom,

the power and the glory,

for ever and ever.

Amen.

In this chapter, I address how the practice of prayer nudges us into an engagement with justice issues by examining the prayer that Jesus taught us to pray. Traditional recitations of prayers can lose their potency and become stale. One way to keep the practice of prayer fresh is to pay attention to the words and their meanings in the prayer. I also propose in this chapter an exercise to expand the words in the recited prayer. If practiced regularly in community, such attention and this exercise can form us and cultivate our imagination so that when big moments for justice engagement come, we are better equipped to act.

Learning to Pray Together: The Church as Parent

In response to our human diversity, multiple forms of prayer evolved over millennia around the globe. Yet the fact that human communities have prayed has not changed; there is constancy in prayer. The exhortation in the first letter to Thessalonians is at the same time an acknowledgement of a deep human truth—that we are drawn to "pray without ceasing" (5: 17).

Such praying can and does happen in solitary settings and is an important spiritual discipline. Jesus went out alone to pray and also instructed his disciples to pray in solitude:

> And whenever you pray, do not be like the hypocrites; for they love to stand and pray in the synagogues and at the street corners, so that they may be seen by others. Truly I tell you, they have received their reward. But whenever you pray, go into your room and shut the door and pray to your Father who is in secret; and your Father who sees in secret will reward you. (Matthew 6:5–6)

Though solitude invites praying, though prayer encourages solitude, and the two are friendly companions, the kind of praying that I am talking about here is prayer practiced as a communal sharing. The Lord's Prayer is a relational prayer. All referents in the Prayer are "our" and not "my," "us" and not "me" only. The Prayer addresses concerns about social life and healing broken relationships among people and communities.

I am particularly interested in this prayer in relation to parenting wisdom gleaned from my children's lived experience, captured in the opening story. Noah and Hannah did not learn this prayer at home. They did not learn this prayer from their parents. It was the church that taught them to learn and memorize this prayer—a church diverse in its members' ages and abilities, appearances and family compositions. Many parents who work outside the home (and, as the recent pandemic has taught us, also plenty of those who work from home) struggle to find adequate time to teach their children. Without supportive social nets including intergenerational support, much learning that children need to become fully human remains undone. Similarly, Christian education should never be the sole responsibility of stereotypical parents in a nuclear family. Moreover, parenting does not happen only at home. In the case of my children, the teaching of the practice of prayer happened at church. My conversation with Hannah and Noah made me realize that the church played a parenting role in teaching them one of the most basic practices of our religious tradition.

This notion of the church as parent is one worth pondering further. I wonder: Can the church be parents in a broad sense of Christian chosen family where different generations teach one another the lessons of faith and life? Where do you notice the church doing parenting? In what ways does this parenting contribute to global justice? To explore these questions, it is helpful to look at two verses of the Prayer that directly address justice in the kingdom (realm/ reign) of God.

Learning the Lord's Prayer

The Prayer contains as many as seven different aspects of prayer: (1) praise and (2) ascriptions of holiness to God *(Hallowed be thy name)*; (3) glorification of God in heaven, the realm of the divinity

(Thine is the kingdom, the power and the glory); (4) confession and (5) a plea for forgiveness *(Forgive us our trespasses, as we forgive those who trespass against us)*; (6) naming human fallibility *(Lead us not into temptation, but deliver from evil)*; (7) a request and yearning for a new world *(Thy kingdom come. Thy will be done, on earth as it is in heaven. Give us this day our daily bread)*.

Among all these important qualities of the Prayer, here I focus on the seventh aspect of prayer, which is about asking and yearning.

"Your Kingdom come. Your will be done, on earth as it is in heaven" (Matthew 6:10). This section of the Prayer prompts us to work for justice to transform our current world into the world God desires. This eschatological vision we behold through our communal practice. The big things are accomplished through small things—that is, by focusing our attention on daily needs. The Prayer asks God to give us what we—the whole community and not only I—need. (*Give us this day our daily bread,* Matthew 6:11).

What stands out to me here is the word "earth" in the petition "Your kingdom come. Your will be done, on earth as it is in heaven." In Greek, "earth" means the current world. In Korean translation, it is literally "land," referring to the entire creation. The word "earth" makes us think of the planet Earth. It reminds us to see the current world in a cosmic way. The environmental challenges facing our world today make it especially critical to look at the Prayer this way. When we pray, "Thy will be done on earth," we reiterate that what God desires for this world is not for the human race only. God's will reaches out to the ends of the earth, and to all the fish, the trees, the water, and the air in it. The Prayer in this section is anchored in justice around the globe. God's will does not have national borders. God's will will be done not in only one part of the world. May God's will be done on the entire planet Earth in the same way as it is done in God's realm, heaven!

And what are we to make of the next phrase—the request for us to be given our daily bread or food?

My immediate family is interracial and interlingual, and this has given me particular insight into this part of the Prayer. It is not unusual to hear us speaking in Korean, even if our dominant language is English.

Growing up, our daughter's favorite bedtime story was *Anne of Green Gables*. Her dad read to her the English version of the *Anne* series by Lucy Maud Montgomery. When she was old enough to read Korean by herself, we bought her a Korean translation. Hannah has read both English and Korean versions at least twice by herself. Partly because of this, Hannah has developed a deep appreciation for how languages translate.

Unlike the Prayer that was taught at the church or by the church intergenerational family, it was I who taught the Korean version of the Prayer to our family at home. When it was time to learn the section "Give us this day our daily bread," we had a lively conversation about the translation of the word "bread." In Korean the word was *yangsik. Yangsik* is how Koreans pronounce 糧食 , which is an East Asian ideogram that means "food." The first character, 糧 , includes 米, meaning rice.[29]

Rice is a staple food of most people on earth. Of the ten most populated countries in the world, which together account for 55 percent of the world's entire population, people there eat rice as their daily food (China, India, Pakistan, Bangladesh, Philippines, Indonesia, Nigeria, Ethiopia, and Egypt, to just name a few). It is true that globalization has brought Western food such as hamburgers, pizza, and pasta to every part of the world. Although the consumption of rice has fallen as a result, it is fair to say that most people living in the Global South, including East and South Asia as well as Africa, still eat rice as their core staple or daily food. Even in Canada, especially in cities such as Toronto and Vancouver where the so-called visible minorities are more than half of the population, many of these immigrants eat rice daily.

In terms of the English translation of the Prayer, "daily bread" refers not to "bread" literally but to staple food. Even though it was not the same kind of bread that Europeans eat, the people who lived in Jesus' time must have eaten bread as well. The Greek word in this prayer, *arton,* is also translated as "bread." Jesus most likely spoke

---

[29]HyeRan Kim-Cragg, *Story and Song: A Postcolonial Interplay between Christian Education and Worship* (New York: Peter Lang, 2012), chap. 6. Anscar J. Chupungco, *Liturgical Inculturation: Sacramentals, Religiosity, and Catechesis* (Collegeville, MI: Liturgical Press, 1992).

Aramaic. The word he used, then, would have been *lakhma* (*lechem* in Hebrew).[30]

"Bread" in the Prayer refers to staple food, to what meets the basic needs of the people.

How do we take these lessons and put them into daily communal practice for a better world? Prayer is mere lip service and ritual unless it leads to action. How are our petitions for a new world and daily food for all to become a reality? How does the Christian practice of the Lord's Prayer in Matthew 6:10–11 relate to the work of parenting and the commitment to global, ecological, and economic justice?

Confessing "God Is Rice!" and Committing Ourselves to Work for Justice

"Thy will [God's will] be done, on earth as it is in heaven. Give us this day our daily bread [daily food]." We recite the Prayer regularly every Sunday. Even in Bible study or special meetings, many Christians gather and disperse with the Prayer. You might say that this Prayer is in the Christian DNA. This part of the Prayer orients us to God who desires a world that is like the world in heaven. God wants the created world to be the world of the divine where the God of justice reigns. In a world of ecological crisis, Christians need to go beyond an androcentric (male), anthropocentric (human), and Eurocentric (white) God. The Lord's Prayer, "Thy kingdom come, thy will be done, on earth as it is heaven," turns to a God beyond the white male and human-centered divinity. To tackle the ecological crisis, we need a different image of God, a different theology. In order to dream a different world, we need different words, different stories.

One image of God that might help decenter androcentric, anthropocentric, and Eurocentric categories is the image of God as rice. The late Japanese theologian Masao Takenaka (竹中正夫)wrote a thought-provoking book with that title: *God Is Rice*.[31] As a social ethicist

---

[30]A. Baadsgaard, "A Taste of Women's Sociality: Cooking as Cooperative Labor in Iron Age Syro-Palestine," in *The World of Women in the Ancient and Classical Near East*, ed. B. A. Nakhai (Newcastle upon Tyne: Cambridge Scholars, 2008), 13–44. Magon Broshi, *Bread, Wine, Walls and Scrolls*, Journal for the Study of the Pseudepigrapha Supplement Series 36 (Sheffield: Sheffield Academic Press, 2001).

[31]Masao Takenaka, *God Is Rice: Asian Culture and Christian Faith* (Geneva: WCC Publications, 1986).

and activist, Takenaka made a major contribution to the indigenization of Christianity in Japan and Asia. This theology of God taps into the deep and wide reservoir of wisdom coming from Asian cultural and ethnic traditions, especially the Korean, Chinese, and Japanese streams of knowledge and language. This is more than a visual idea because what rice represents is more than an image: It is a way of life, particularly through the acts of "eating," "growing," and "sharing."

Similarly thought-provoking is a poem called "Rice Is Heaven," written by Korean intellectual and Christian activist Kim Jiha, who was imprisoned for fighting for democracy under the military regime of Park Jeong-Hee in the 1970s. Here, heaven has a theological connotation, very much in line with the view of the gospel of Matthew. Takenaka cites Kim Jiha's poem in his book as well:

Heaven is rice

As we cannot go to heaven alone

We should share rice with one another

As all share the light of the heavenly stars

We should share and eat rice together

Heaven is rice

When we eat and swallow rice

Heaven dwells in our body

Rice is heaven

Yes, rice is the matter

We should eat together[32]

Takenaka's claim that God is rice should not be understood literally, of course. It is a metaphor. Rice and God are not exactly the same thing. Rather, his claim underscores that rice is an indigenous Asian symbol of God's gift of both earthly and eternal life. To say that God is rice is to understand rice as a metaphorical and material source of meaning connected to the whole of God's creation. It proclaims that God invites us to be in harmonious, just, and nourishing relationships

[32]Kim Jiha, "Rice Is Heaven," *Pab: A Collection* (Seoul: Paulist, 1986).

with all of nature. When we preach the good news that "God is rice," we are proclaiming our just relationships with the land, the Earth, the whole creation. When we confess that God is rice or that heaven is rice, we are also confessing the sovereignty of God as we commit ourselves to making sure that rice is shared equitably so that no one goes hungry in the entire world: "Thy will be done on earth as it is in heaven. Give us this day our daily bread."

Whenever we proclaim together with our children that God is rice or that heaven is rice, and whenever we recite the Prayer "Give us this day our daily bread," we are joining the global justice movement and committing ourselves to communal and relational equity work. Growing rice requires good relationships with people, strong and healthy social networks, and practices of negotiation and coalition so that the benefit of rice can be shared peacefully and equitably. This Asian indigenous theology invites us, adults and children alike, to embrace and imagine God as something as expansive as the land itself.

Kim Jiha's prophetic poem "Rice Is Heaven" helps us to tap into decolonial thinking and practice that addresses economic justice. It challenges the profit-driven neoliberal capitalist system by insisting that rice cannot be commodified and privatized. It reminds us that rice is not something to fill up the stomachs only of the most powerful, but that it must be shared and protected for the sake of feeding the hungry.

Finally, this indigenous theology, from Japan and Korea, of God as rice contests androcentric, anthropocentric, Eurocentric Western imperial theology that portrays God as white and enthroned alone in heaven, looking down indifferently from the sky. Instead, this image of God as rice encourages us to pray earnestly, "Give us this day our daily bread [rice/food]," by entertaining and evoking the holy one who works in the rice field, cooperating to grow food to feed the hungry and to bring "thy kingdom...on earth as it is in heaven."

Expanding the Lord's Prayer

The practice of praying together forms us as collective and moral agents. When we pray as a family (church, nuclear, or otherwise), we encourage one another to act for the well-being of the community. The Lord's Prayer has an eschatological vision, a vision that is not within our immediate grasp. Thus, when we pray this Prayer, it stretches us to expand our imagination to embrace the alternative reality that is coming. To live a different world, we must imagine that world.

The following expanded Lord's Prayer does that. This is the prayer practiced during the World Alliance of Reformed Churches (WARC) General Council in Accra, Ghana in 2004. It is the so-called "Accra Prayer."[33] It was written based on the Prayer with a special eye to global justice, especially economic justice. I am sharing this prayer as a concrete example of the forward-moving global justice practice of prayer that is pregnant with imagination and also taps into concrete and current reality.

I highlight in italics the section of the Lord's Prayer I examined in this article.

> Our Father who art in heaven, Beloved God, Creator of heaven and earth, and of all the peoples of the earth, bring peace and righteousness to all the peoples. In your grace, may equity grow. Turn our hearts to you in healing and transformation.

> Hallowed be thy name. Be present to all peoples, that we may open our eyes and recognize you in our history, in our cultures, in our struggles. Deliver us from enchantment by the false gods of money, markets, and status.

> Help us to praise you in our faith and actions, that, seeing our loving service in your name, others, too, may bless that name. *Thy kingdom come.* Where people resist injustice, live in solidarity, and seek a more human social order, help us to recognize the ferment of your kingdom already at work. Bless those who are poor, those who suffer for the sake of justice, those who promote and defend human rights. Bless the children of our countries, and protect them from terror and oppression.

> *Thy will be done.* Yes! That your wisdom would be our wisdom! Deliver us from adjusting to unjust systems. Move our hearts, and the hearts of women and men everywhere, to act in love, that we may resist the seductions of power and greed and may live in right relationships with all. *[O]n earth*

---

[33]See "The ACCRA Confession," http://wcrc.ch/accra/the-accra-confession. The prayer is used with permission.

as it is in heaven. God, present in every movement of creation, let us be responsible stewards of your garden of life, striving for sustainability. And as the firmament in all its mystery and glory displays your cosmic will, so may our lives display the mystery and glory of love, your will for life on earth.

Give us this day our daily bread. That no one may be threatened by hunger, malnutrition, or scarcity, give bread to those who have none and hunger for justice to those who have bread. Teach us what is enough for today, and to share with those who have less than enough, for in this, it is Jesus whom we serve. And forgive us our debts. Don't let us lose our lives, as persons and as peoples, because of our debts. Let not the poorest pay for the benefit of the richest in unfair demands, punitive interest rates, and excessive charges. But forgive us, and let justice prevail, as we forgive our debtors.

As we live by your grace and sharing of your very self, deliver us from systems of aggressive and divisive individualism. Break our chains of selfishness, open our hearts to those who need our solidarity, and deliver us from illusion, that we might practice what we preach. And lead us not into temptation, but deliver us from being bewitched by power, and keep us faithful to you; for you are our help, where else can we appeal.

Money will not save us, nor the market, nor our powerful friends. Strengthen us to resist the false attraction of easy answers, magic fixes, abuses of power, and the delusion that there is any way apart from justice in which God's justice can be done. But deliver us from evil.

From every evil that objectifies the earth, all living beings, and our neighbours; from every evil that degrades creation and destroys societies; from every evil that encourages us to think that we are God.

So may we learn from you to refrain from judgment, to accord respect to all God's creation, and so be privileged to hear the witness of those the world treats with indignity. Because yours is the kingdom, the power and the glory, for ever and ever. Amen.

Try It Out

If you have memorized the Prayer, it may be a fruitful practice among your home and church families to expand the Prayer in a way that reflects your current context, including but not limited to economic and ecological issues, while yearning for a new world to come.

- Talk to your children or your family members about the Prayer, where and how each of you learned it.

- With one another, share the particular phrase in the Prayer that speaks to your heart most powerfully, and explain why. This sharing could be done as a communal session in the congregation beyond home settings.

- Expand the Prayer in your own words, using the Accra prayer above or any other prayer[34] as an example. You might write different versions on newsprint and illustrate it. Be bold in stretching your imagination, and be specific in creating this expansive action-oriented prayer toward global justice as something we can do as a daily practice.

---

[34]The Lord's Prayer from the *New Zealand Prayer Book* is another excellent example that focuses on ecological concern using inclusive God language. https://kathwilliamson.blogspot.com/2009/05/lords-prayer-from-new-zealand.html

5

Give Back Packs

Ellen Ott Marshall with Carlton Mackey and Isaiah Mackey

Ten-year old Isaiah is standing at a counter filling large plastic bags with one pair of socks, peanut butter crackers, nutrition bars, and a bottle of water. He will put these bags in the back of his dad's car to hand out to people asking for help on the side of the road. Isaiah calls these bags "Give Back Packs," and they represent his commitment to giving 10 percent of his earnings to help people in need. The Give Back Packs are also one part of a larger lesson that Isaiah is learning about developing a healthy relationship with possessions. Isaiah's dad, Carlton, learned this lesson from his parents and grandparents and is eager to pass it on. In doing so, he is also intentionally challenging tropes of Black men as either poor or flaunting their wealth or as absent from their children's lives altogether. Resisting tropes like this is a central commitment of Carlton's and the purpose of the platform he created, called Black Men Smile®.

This chapter invites you into a conversation with Carlton and Isaiah. They focus on two interrelated challenges: cultivating a healthy relationship with possessions, and resisting the images that society projects onto Black men. Black Men Smile® is their response to both of these challenges. As a platform, it celebrates the way Black men see themselves. As an entrepreneurial business in which Isaiah participates, it provides an opportunity for him to learn about saving, spending, earning, and giving.

Black Men Smile

Carlton: So I am the creator of a platform that is a vehicle for resistance and activism. I believe in leveraging the power of art to effect social change, and I am also aware of and understand the power of media (and social media in particular) to communicate ideas, to transfer knowledge, and to inspire action. The mission of Black Men Smile® is to celebrate the way we see ourselves. It is rooted in the notion that "the revolution begins when the something you believe in is you." Black Men Smile® is centered on these ideas of radical self-love and joy. These are revolutionary acts, particularly in environments where you are not invited to celebrate yourself, or to have or express joy, or to take up space. This is the idea that Black Men Smile® was built upon.

As a parent, I began to realize the difference between how I wanted Isaiah to perceive himself and what the narrative may be about him. Although Isaiah is not allowed to have his own social media accounts, he's already a consumer of digital media. He is consuming information that has the power to shape his identity.

There are tropes of Black men and Black identity: as hyper-sexualized, aggressive, violent, and lazy. There's also this idea of having (particularly in certain aspects of hip-hop culture) and of flaunting what we have. I understand that some of that may be a response to having to go without. Spending on Jordans or flashy cars or whatever it is may be a response to so often having so little. I don't want Isaiah to have a mentality of lack or of scarcity. But at the same time, I don't want him to feel that having makes him any better than anyone else. I also don't want him to develop this notion that we have to outwardly express what we have as a rebuttal to the notion that we don't.

So this work that we are talking about with you is a counter to that, and it matches directly with the work of Black Men Smile® because I understand fundamentally that among the things we are doing—and not for other people but for ourselves—is challenging the way we think about ourselves and rejecting the notion that how we think about ourselves has to be simply based on ideas that are projected onto us. This allows for Isaiah to begin to see himself in these platforms in a positive way.

Black Dads Matter

Soon, Isaiah was not only absorbing positive images, but designing them. Isaiah's first shirt, a "statement Tee," came about because of his involvement in an activity that was part of an exhibit at the High Museum in Atlanta, Georgia. Isaiah and Carlton tell the story.

Isaiah: So there was an event at the High Museum and they wanted people to write something motivational.

Carlton energetically interrupts to provide some context: Oh sorry. I gotta say this because it's so important. Protest! The event was centered on an exhibit that—I can't think of the name of the artist—but it was of Tommie Smith, who was the Black athlete. Tommie Smith and Juan Carlos at the 1967 Olympics raised their fists in protest. It was a memorial to that event and to Tommie Smith. And the High Museum of Art had an event, as a part of the community engagement around the exhibit. They were talking about art and its connection to protest. They had pre-cut poster boards that you could use to make protest signs, and a sub-set of them would be chosen to put on display in the exhibit.

Isaiah: Um, so, I was told to write something motivational, and I asked my dad for help because I just didn't know what to write. And he said that I should write something that Martin Luther King, Jr., would say. And I was thinking in my head and I wanted to say something that could help people to not compare themselves to others and think that they're better than they are for certain reasons. So, I decided to write that "You are the best you."

Carlton: And I took a picture of that poster. We left it at the High because you were supposed to. But I took a picture of it on my phone and had it turned into a print that I put on a shirt that I gave to Isaiah. And I think I wore it or he wore it and someone said, "Oh, I like that. Where did you get that?" And I thought, Oh, of course! Isaiah, you might be onto something.

Isaiah's second shirt design came around Father's Day when he created a shirt for Carlton that read "Black Dads Matter" and gave it to him as a Father's Day present. Like "You are the best you," they started making more of these shirts and selling them. Suddenly, Isaiah was making money.

Isaiah: It was around Father's Day of 2020, I made a shirt called "Black Dads Matter" and it was a gray sweatshirt. I just started making a lot of money, and I couldn't just use all that money for myself.

When Isaiah started earning money from his own shirt designs, then Black Men Smile® became not only a platform informing his image of himself, but also a space where he could learn a healthy relationship with possessions. For Carlton, Isaiah's involvement as an entrepreneur with Black Men Smile® opened up the chance to help his son develop financial literacy (and practice math). So, Carlton introduced a budget plan for Isaiah to follow: 40, 40, 10, 10. He can spend 40 percent of what he makes, but he also needs to save 40 percent, invest 10 percent back into the business, and give 10 percent to others.

Carlton: One of the lessons and values that I want to instill in Isaiah is a healthy relationship with money. This includes the lessons of philanthropy, of giving back, of the spiritual concept of tithing, and also of basic financial literacy. The financial literacy part of this is important because we live in a capitalist world that's driven as much as anything by finances. And how we manage and use them, how we leverage and understand money and concepts around money is one of the most important lessons we can learn and, I would argue, one of the least-taught lessons that we have in our formal education. And so what I want to instill in Isaiah is a number of things. One is that you have the ability to use your brain and your creativity to be a source of income for yourself. I want to instill in him this idea around creative capitalism—that we can be conscious and responsible with how we make money and with how we utilize it. We can also use our minds and our creativity to address problems, which is, I think, a fundamental concept behind any successful entrepreneurial endeavor. It addresses problems, and it allows us to live out our passion while seeking a purpose.

I want him to see and understand the value of money and what it can allow him to do and to possess while not having a hoarding mentality or a scarcity mentality.

Carlton turns to Isaiah to ask: What was one of the most significant things that you bought?

Isaiah: Well, the GoPro, um...and the other thing I think was, oh, the Oculus.

Carlton adds: And tons of Fortnite cards.

Carlton: So there is this idea that you can have things, and I will not always be your sole provider. You are a resource unto yourself, and you can have some of the things that you desire by your willingness to work and earn them. But there is also a commitment and a responsibility to earning money, which is to have a healthy relationship with it. And part of that healthy relationship is built around this idea of these four buckets that I conceptualized. He can spend 40 percent of what he earns, but he also has to save 40 percent, invest 10 percent, and give 10 percent.

It's a math lesson, to be honest, because he has to calculate what the percentages are. So, it's a math lesson; it's a lesson in entrepreneurship; it's a lesson in financial literacy. He has to do the math to determine how much goes into each of these four buckets.

Back to that relationship with money: You have a responsibility to that which you are given to give. You also have a responsibility to that which you earn to save. But you also have the luxury, by working hard and earning, to reward and treat yourself. It is highly valuable to me for him to understand that he is worthy of pursuing his desires and seeing that he can reach goals that he sets. Money is a means for him to live out some of his dreams, but that is not its sole purpose.

It's important that he is allowed to build wealth himself so that he experiences being able to have and possess things because he wants them. It doesn't have to be outlandish to work and go get something that's very expensive. But because it's matched with an equal commitment to give back and an equal commitment to save, an equal understanding that he earned it, but he has to invest back in the company to get more. I think these ideas [I'm teaching him] are counter to the ideas that may shape his understanding in a negative way.

A Legacy of Giving

Carlton: The idea behind the 10 percent is very much a spiritual concept that was instilled in me by my parents. The idea was as much a way to honor lessons that I have taken with me as it was to honor my dad and my grandma who believed in the spiritual concept of giving a tithe. They anchored it to Scripture. "Will anyone rob God? [Yes, in his] tithes and offerings" (Malachi 3:8). I can remember that Bible verse because I heard them say that. "[T]o whom much has been given, much will be required" (Luke 12:48). They tithed to the church to do the work of the Lord. It's the idea that we are to be stewards of that which is given to us. To open up the possibility of receiving blessings, we must give. For Isaiah, it was about carrying on that legacy.

Though I haven't used that language of "tithe" with Isaiah, this percentage and idea is centered on or rooted in this kind of social justice, of activism, of narrowing the distance, which is something he's heard me say before. Seeking to get closer, to seek understanding from that which we do not understand: All of these things are part of the principle of giving now. It is a principle of mine that I shared with him, because it was a principle that was shared with me. And it's of even greater value [to me] now because I lost my father recently. And it's beautiful...that this is a lifestyle of giving and of giving back that is being instilled in Isaiah. And that is also as much the purpose of this practical idea. It has spiritual and personal and familial legacy concepts behind it as well.

My parents would talk about this idea of giving as a way of making a way, of clearing a pathway to receive. But it wasn't giving just to get back. In their own way, they were talking about having healthy relationships with our possessions.

Isaiah has clearly been formed in this legacy of giving.

Isaiah: I started making shirts, and I just started making a lot of money. And when that happened, I couldn't just spend all my money on myself, and I needed to do different things with it. So, I decided to do these Give Back Packs because I always was sad when we had no money to give to people who asked for help, and I wanted to give them something. So, we just decided to go and buy these items and put them in the bag and then give them to people.

Give Back Packs

Ellen: How old were you when you started doing this?

Isaiah: I think it was last year, when I came up with a new shirt idea. And I started making way more money than the shirt I made before. So I have four things I split the money into. I would spend it on investing into the company. I would put 10 percent of the money into that. I would put 40 percent to spend on myself. I would put 40 percent into savings. And I would put 10 percent into the Give Back Packs.

Carlton: What is a Give Back Pack?

Isaiah: The Give Back Packs are like…um, they're used for people who don't have as much, people who don't have a home and are maybe hungry. And we give them these things so that they can eat and have better socks. So, just to help them out a little bit. In the Give Back Packs we put some socks, water, and food. Like chips and nutrition bars, and I think the other thing was fruit snacks.

Carlton: I know we give KIND® bars or the nutritional bars, as you said. Do we consistently put peanut butter crackers in them?

Isaiah: Yes, that is another thing. So, a lot of food.

Isaiah: We did used to put dollars in them. I don't remember why we stopped doing that, but we used to put $1 in every one.

Ellen: Was it hard for you to decide what to put in the Give Back Packs?

Isaiah: Me and my dad were just talking about what we should put in them, and we just decided that they should have socks, and definitely water. Because that is an essential thing, and a lot of food, so they can have a lot of food for at least a couple of days, to help them out, and $1 that they could just spend on anything that will help them.

Ellen: Tell me a little about the process of shopping and putting them together.

Isaiah: We go out with the money that I put aside for them. We go to the store, and we purchase all those items, all those goods, and then we put one bag of chips, a bar, um, some fruit snacks, some socks, a bottle of water, and then we used to put $1 in there. And we put them in our car; and whenever someone is asking for money on the side of the road, we give them one of those bags.

Carlton: We keep the Give Back Packs on the backseat with Isaiah. Let's say we are approaching a red light, and people come to the driver's side window asking for something. I won't roll down the driver's side window. I'll roll down the backseat window, and they'll look and then they'll kind of slide to the back. It's Isaiah's face they see. And he grabs a bag and he hands them a Give Back Pack.

When we don't have a Give Back Pack, you know, we offer a word of encouragement, we try to make eye contact, we say something; but in most cases when we don't have Give Back Packs, we don't give anything. And we're always reminded when we don't have anything to give—it's a really interesting cycle—we come home and think, Dang, we've got to make more Give Back Packs.

Ellen: I came into this interview assuming that the challenge that we'd be focusing on would be related to disrupting the narratives about Black men. And I think that's still a part of the conversation. But I find myself focusing on this challenge of helping our kids develop a healthy relationship with possessions.

Carlton: It's there. It's a pillar of this conversation. Both in terms of what I value and what I want to uplift. For sure, I am a Black man, and I'm raising someone, a son, who I want to engage in the world in a certain way, with a certain kind of confidence, and who I want to see me in a certain way. But for sure I am trying to instill in him lessons about our relationship with things, our relationship with money, our relationship with possessions, our relationship with work—you know, all these things.

Ellen: So there is the challenge of helping kids develop a healthy relationship with possessions; and there is the challenge of helping Isaiah develop a healthy self-image, which entails resisting some projections onto him and providing him with affirming images of Black men. It's striking to me that Black Men

Smile® has provided a practice that addresses both of these challenges: providing Isaiah with positive images and bringing him into the business so that he can learn these important lessons about entrepreneurship, financial literacy, and tithing. All of this comes together in the video you filmed of Isaiah shopping and assembling the Give Back Packs. Can you say a little more about the purpose of that video?

Carlton: So this platform was largely built around the idea that you can communicate ideas to transfer knowledge and inspire action. Making the video is about realizing that sharing it can inspire action by others. It can catalyze action, but it can also just inspire people. [The Give Back Pack] was an idea that we created and do, but we also understand the power that it is to bear witness to a truth. And that truth is that we can take action; we can do things to challenge our perceptions of ourselves and the other; we can—even if small—make a difference; we can shift the narrative that we have among ourselves about who we are, as Black men. We can, through leveraging the power of social media, bear witness to that truth and show others who we are as Black men, who we are as Black fathers, who we are as human beings.

There are little things we can do. The video and leveraging the power of social media was a vehicle for us to do that. Black Men Smile® is about sharing stories. Black Men Smile® is about celebrating the way we see ourselves. It is about valuing our story over and above the narratives and the stories that people tell about us. And it's powerful to hear responses of people who say, "I saw your video, and I was inspired to action. I saw your video, and I was encouraged to know that what I may have thought or heard about Black men and Black fathers, isn't fundamentally or inevitably true."

Ellen: So how do you feel when you give these Packs out?

Isaiah: I feel, um, I just feel mostly proud that I did that. When I hand the bags to people, they're always grateful and just thankful and appreciative, and they just say thank you so much; and it just makes me feel better.

Try It Out

- Set aside 10 percent of any money you receive to give to others.

- Get gallon-size plastic bags and items that would be useful to the people you want to help. We use bottles of water, socks, nutrition bars, peanut butter crackers, and sometimes $1 bills.

- Fill each bag and keep them with you as you drive around town.

- When you come across people asking for help, give them a Give Back Pack.

6

Interruptive Listening

Luke Larner

My son was about three years old the first time he gently placed his hand on my shoulder and calmly said, "Daddy, just listen a minute, please!" He has done this many more times since. Such moments of interruption, both funny and painful, are opportunities for reflection (and sometimes repentance). I'm on a lifelong journey of trying to learn the art of listening and the art of good interruption—and in this chapter I want to encourage you to join me in cultivating this art. These two skills are essential because the struggle for justice is built on the way we relate to others. For a penitent motor-mouth like me, it is a daily struggle. But I have come to realize that learning and modeling interruptive listening for our children is one way in which we, as parents, can work toward the flourishing of our society and world within the course of our daily lives.

Some years ago I was part of a Christian motorcycle club. One evening, I was on bar duty after a long and eventful ride up to the clubhouse in the North West of England. One of our guests was a grizzled biker with quite the reputation. He approached the bar and, respecting biker club culture, turned to a senior member of my club and asked if it was okay to "teach the new lad a few things." Obliging him, the senior member turned to me and said words I will never forget: "You've got two ears and one mouth. Act accordingly."

What followed was an incredibly intimate moment of human connection. The grizzled biker shared his life story, moments of incredible pain and regret, and how, having read the Bible cover to cover in prison, he was now certain that Jesus' words "You will be with me in paradise" applied to him too. I could have judged him, tried to force a tract into his hand, or tried to convince him with the best arguments from contemporary apologetics. If I had done any of those, I would have left not only with a broken nose but also having missed a very special moment of connection that I will carry with me forever. Years later as a chapter president in the motorcycle club, I often joked that there are many transferrable skills between club life, justice work, and parenting a toddler, not least careful listening and negotiation.

What Is Interruptive Listening?

Listening is such a basic virtue that many of us have already had its necessity drilled into us by the time we start school. But as my son showed me in the example I gave earlier, it's not enough to tell children to listen: We have to model this in our interactions with them. Kids don't respond well to "Do as I say, not as I do." In fact, "the kinds of relationship they experience will lay the groundwork for how they relate to others for the rest of their lives."[35]

I'm using the term *listening* cautiously, given its potential to exclude those with hearing loss, so I want to clarify that by listening I mean the sort of intentional pause in communication that allows us to connect properly with people, be it our children, our friends, or our allies in the fight for justice. I'm using the term *interruptive listening* because listening in itself is not enough. Sometimes it can feel as if people are listening to us when in reality they are trying to figure us out to suit their own agendas.[36] Market research is a kind of listening, but it is not an *interruptive* listening. The term *interruptive listening* might seem like an oxymoron or a contradiction in terms. Isn't listening the opposite of interrupting? My own daily battle with hyperactivity

---

[35]Daniel J. Siegel and Tina Payne Bryson, *The Whole-Brain Child: 12 Revolutionary Strategies to Nurture Your Child's Developing Mind* (New York: Bantam Books, 2012), 125.

[36]See Al Barrett and Ruth Harley, *Being Interrupted: Reimagining the Church's Mission from the Outside, In* (London: SCM Press, 2020).

and attention deficit makes the desire to interrupt overwhelming sometimes, especially when I become energized and excited by what people are saying to me. Interruptive listening is a beautiful collision of opposites, a two-way street that allows our own agendas to be interrupted and acknowledges the interruptive presence of others.

Interruptive listening means pausing one's own agenda and desire to speak in order to attend fully to the other person. Henri Nouwen regards this as one of the most powerful acts of hospitality and love that we can show to one another.[37] In justice work I have repeatedly seen well-intentioned people allow their *help* to turn into *hurt* because they couldn't see past their own agenda. They couldn't let their own plans be interrupted enough to *see* and *hear* the people they were trying to support. This, of course, relates to parenting too. I try (and often fail) to make my son feel heard and valued, especially when he's distressed. I also try to ask him good questions. I want him to learn that listening is an act of love.

Interruptive listening also acknowledges that not all outside interruptions are bad. As a cheeky and chatty working-class person ministering in a formal and middle-class denomination, sometimes my mere presence in the room can feel like an interruption or disruption. I feel this bodily too. Artist Grayson Perry describes how a tattooed working-class body like mine shaped by a decade of hard labor as a bricklayer can seem "chaotic" compared to the "buttoned up middle-class body." For those of us with one or more intersections of identity that contrast us with what Perry calls the "default man," our very presence can interrupt.[38]

Yet both the interruption of our personal agendas and the interrupting presence of others are key in both justice work and parenting. The strange web of lack and privilege I bring into my own work continues to show me both sides of this. I've met so many people who have felt disempowered and badly done-to not only by systems, structures, and institutions, but also by their main caregivers. This limits their sense of agency and needs to be interrupted. In his book *Poverty Safari*, Scottish rapper Darren McGarvey describes the anger of people living in struggling estates/housing projects when so-called

[37]Henri J. M. Nouwen, *The Wounded Healer: Ministry in Contemporary Society* (New York: Image Books, 1990), 89.

[38]Grayson Perry, *The Descent of Man* (London: Penguin Books, 2017), 67.

professionals swoop in to save the day without taking the time to listen to the wisdom and experiences of local people. They just as quickly depart, having achieved little more than something notable to put on their LinkedIn profiles.[39] This is a problematic dynamic I frequently observe among charities and Christian churches and para-church organizations. Despite their good intentions, they think they know better than the local communities they seek to serve, especially children. It's not enough to listen to people and then to try to be a so-called voice for the voiceless. As Arundhati Roy notes, "There's really no such thing as the 'voiceless.' There are only the deliberately silenced, or the preferably unheard."[40] The pain of struggling communities and particularly suffering children should not be a commodity for activists to exploit. It's clear that there are good reasons that tensions can arise between well-meaning Christians and the communities they try to serve.

I've been guilty of this myself.

Allowing our agendas to be interrupted and seeing the interruptive presence of the other as a gift are both important tasks in parenting. To raise happy, secure children, we cannot allow them to be crushed by our agendas or to experience constant rejection through our anger or annoyance at their interruptions. While boundaries are important, I've known enough children of Christian leaders to be aware of the harm that parents with dominant personalities and busy schedules can do. There needs to be some consistency in how we show up for our families and how we show up for the communities we serve and the justice movements to which we belong—and we need to practice interruptive listening in all these arenas.

Seen And Not Heard?

The expectation that children should be seen and not heard has often characterized parenting and work with children and young people. One of the old books my kid inherited tells the story of a monster eating a child because he'd interrupted so much that his parents stopped listening. I wonder what message that sends to a developing

---

[39]Darren McGarvey, *Poverty Safari: Understanding the Anger of Britain's Underclass,* paperback ed. (London: Picador, 2018), 76.

[40]Arundhati Roy, *The Ordinary Person's Guide to Empire* (London: Harper Perennial, 2004), 330.

mind. Children and young people often feel unheard and lacking in agency. Yet many show remarkable wisdom and insight about the world, which they are often willing to share in a safe, well-facilitated space. Frustrating as it can be sometimes, the interruptions I receive from my own son (who is five at the time of writing) can be just the interruption I need. Jared is a deep thinker, and he often has really fascinating ideas and thoughts. His reflections on God, prayer, and some of the children's books we have read on these topics have often challenged my own theology. The temptation here is to correct him with the "right" answer, but I think that would not only disempower him, it would also mean missing the chance for my own thoughts to be valuably interrupted. From a young age he began to question big theological ideas such as omnipotence by reflecting on his own experiences of unanswered prayers—questions with which I have wrestled too. Allowing his straightforward approaches to these questions has proven a valuable interruption in my own journey of faith—"out of the mouth of babes…"

A maxim of Community Organising—an approach to pursuing justice explored by Keith and Martha Hebden in this book—is, "Those who are closest to the pain are closest to the solution." So interruptive listening can mean that our so-called good ideas as activists, organizers, youth leaders, and even parents might need some interrupting with the wisdom and experience of the people for whom we are trying to care. Sometimes the interruption is so strong that we just need to stop and let our seemingly bright but frankly misguided ideas fall by the wayside. I'm noticing more and more that what I am learning as a parent and family member is teaching me to be a better justice practitioner by allowing me to be interrupted, and to hold my power and privilege carefully.

Interruption: From Self-Emptying to Non-Grasping

How might we understand interruptive listening theologically? I'm troubled by the way that some Christian literature seems to assume the activist or practitioner is a privileged person who has "lowered themselves" to serve in underprivileged communities. I also worry about the way parenthood is sometimes talked about as a form of sacrifice or even a "cross to bear." These narratives are sometimes based on the teaching of Philippians 2:

Let each of you look not to your own interests, but to the interests of others. Let the same mind be in you that was in Christ Jesus,

who, though he was in the form of God,

did not regard equality with God

as something to be exploited,

but emptied himself,

taking the form of a slave,

being born in human likeness.

And being found in human form,

he humbled himself

and became obedient to the point of death—

even death on a cross.

Therefore God also highly exalted him

and gave him the name

that is above every name,

so that at the name of Jesus

every knee should bend,

in heaven and on earth and under the earth,

and every tongue should confess

that Jesus Christ is Lord,

to the glory of God the Father. (Philippians 2:4–11)

The word often used to describe this is *kenosis*, translated as "self-emptying." It's easy to see how this can apply to activism and mission. I remember once visiting the local Gurdwara with my Sikh neighbor, and he said, "We Sikhs see family life as a gift in the spiritual life, not a hindrance." His words challenged me deeply to look for the ways that I am being formed as a person of faith and a justice practitioner through family life. The Christian might see their service in deprived communities as some sort of self-emptying. Maybe the brave few even sold up and moved their families into the neighborhood—a move some have described as "incarnational ministry." The problem with this is that it assumes God wasn't already there, at work through and in people who are struggling together for the common good. This likewise applies to parenthood: God is at work in and through our children, if only we have "ears to hear." A misguided view of service, activism, and parenthood that fails to see God at work in the "other" can often lead to tensions. Activists and parents alike might start to feel that the people they serve are ungrateful if they don't respond well. The flip side of this is that local people might question the motives of people (maybe people of privilege) who move in to the neighborhood and try to take over or tell people what to do. For example, tensions can arise resulting from contrasting styles of parenting. Again, this is why interruptive listening is so important. We must allow ourselves to be challenged by others at least as much as we seek to challenge. Remember: two ears, one mouth.

Another way of looking at *kenosis* is to see it as non-grasping rather than self-emptying. Reflecting particularly on Philippians 2, theologian Sarah Coakley suggests that rather than self-emptying, we should see Jesus' incarnate life among us as a refusal to grasp certain forms of power.[41] As Christian parents and activists, how might we refuse forms of power or ways of holding power and privilege that oppress rather than liberate? To hold our power lightly with our children is a way to prepare us and them to be a force for good and for liberation in the world.

Reflecting on this theme of *kenosis,* theologian Amaryah Armstrong asks what it might look like to understand *kenosis* as making room for others, particularly those others who are excluded from spaces that the privileged monopolize. She sees it as particularly important to listen to movements that disrupt the status quo and challenge unjust power structures in society, even if they don't come directly from the church. One such example she cites is the Black Lives Matter movement. She describes movements such as BLM as "Spirited interruptions."[42]

[41]Sarah Coakley, *Powers and Submissions: Spirituality, Philosophy, and Gender* (Oxford: Blackwell Publishers, 2002), 11.

[42]Amaryah Jones-Armstrong, "The Spirit and the Subprime: Race, Risk, and Our Common Dispossession," *Anglican Theological Review* 98, no. 1 (2016): 56–58.

So in this sense, our interruptive listening is a *discerning* listening. Interruptive listening means, in the words of missionary Bishop John V. Taylor, to "begin in the beginning with the Holy Spirit." It means to hold our plans lightly that we might discern what She is doing and join in.[43] I've come to the conclusion that *kenosis,* whether in justice work, ministry, or parenting, is only really beneficial when framed in this way—as a *non-grasping* rather than as a *self-emptying.*

The Practice of Interruptive Listening

The practice of interruptive listening is really quite simple: It's about being "quick to listen, slow to speak, slow to anger" (James 1:19). This verse is in the context of a passage about "taming the tongue." In the context of parenting, it sometimes means learning great patience as my son explains his feelings in the roundabout way children do with their limited vocabularies. It means taking the time to stop and reflect on what he says, to try not to over-react or shut him down when I don't like what he says. It means the craft of learning to ask him good questions to help him reflect and clarify his own thoughts. These are all practices that require cultivation, and often rely on a healthy spiritual life. Simple as it may sound, I have found that taking time for daily silence and stillness has a big impact—my family notice when I don't! This, in turn, also flows over into my work as a minister, community organizer, and justice practitioner. I want to be consistent in who I am in and out of the clerical collar, and I'm trying to make interruptive listening a daily habit. Of course, I regularly fail—and sometimes the interruptive listening offers my family the chance to be heard when they want to tell me where I've gone wrong.

How does this practice of interruptive listening—learned and honed in our home lives—translate into our engagement in social justice initiatives? A few years back I helped develop a mentoring program for young men who were at risk of involvement in so-called "knife crime." I personally prefer the term "violence affecting young people," because when children as young as eleven are carrying knives to feel safe, the real crime is that society hasn't done something about it. Many of the young people with whom I spoke shared experiences of incredible pain and trauma, which left them vulnerable to exploitation

---

[43]John V. Taylor, *Go-Between God: New Edition* (London: SCM, 2021), 43.

by adult criminals. The key adults in their lives had written off many of them, and many struggled to get help at a time during which funding for youth services had been slashed. They had not been listened to. So, in response, we decided to try and prioritize listening to them and others. We asked young people how they had been affected, what they thought might produce positive change, and how they might respond creatively. We did the same thing with parents in community groups in the areas most affected. I was bowled over by the wisdom, insight, and resilience of their responses. We decided that as part of our response we wanted to bring people together publicly to change some of the narratives about violence affecting young people, and to let the experiences these young people shared speak for themselves. So, we made a short film so that these experiences could be shared anonymously. We also retrieved about five hundred knives from local amnesty bins, and I helped a design technology teacher friend from church turn these knives into a sculpture of a phoenix. With the help of local church leaders, we managed to convince the shopping mall to let us play our film on their big advertising screen. Then, with a large group of people from the local community, we processed to the steps of the town hall for a peace vigil at which the sculpture was unveiled. As part of the vigil, we painted our hands red to signify that we were not washing our hands clean but instead were accepting that we all have a responsibility for the children in our community. A senior police officer joined us in this ritual, and was visibly moved by it. All of this only emerged through allowing the usual responses to knife crime—those that blame young people—to be interrupted by listening to the voices of those directly involved, those on the inside.

Listening to God

I understand every experience of listening as in some way listening to God, an interruptive listening to the Spirit speaking to me through the people I've met. This, of course, is also true of children, for "it is to such as these that the kingdom of heaven belongs" (Matthew 19:14). I cannot count the number of times children, especially my own son, have prophetically challenged me in a way I can only take as a gift from the Spirit. Children help us see the world through different eyes. One example of this came recently when the UK's Home Office planned to house a large number of people seeking asylum in portacabins adjacent to a notorious immigration removal center, in the middle of a cold winter and a soaring COVID infection rate. I try to avoid taking work calls during family time, but I knew I needed to answer this one. Afterward my son asked me what I had been talking about, and I explained why the call was important enough to take up ten minutes of Saturday morning cartoon time. He became really angry, saying how mean and unkind this was and asking how they would like to be locked up in a place that's cold and like a prison! Sometimes the only way we can be re-sensitized to the injustice in the world is when we glimpse it through the eyes of a child.

One of the ways I like to listen to and be interrupted by God is through engaging with the red letters—the teachings of Jesus printed in red in some versions of the Bible. Two things strike me about Jesus. One, he spent time listening to children, which was pretty radical for his day. He valued children, often using them as an example to follow. And two, like children he asked a *lot* of questions! In fact, Jesus rarely did anything for anyone without asking the question "What do you want me to do for you?" Reflecting on the life of Christ should challenge us as parents to allow our children to minister to us, to challenge us with their interruptions and their questions. If our churches and organizations followed Jesus' example and took the time to build close enough relationships with the people and communities we serve, then we, too, might find the answer to the question "What do you want me to do?"

I've tried to apply this principle in my parenting too: I try to ask questions; I try to ask my son what I can do to help when he is upset, and I really try to listen to his response. I hope that this will both give him a secure sense of self and model what it means to care and love another person. In the ongoing struggle for justice and liberation, we need future generations who know that they have two ears and one mouth, and act accordingly.

Try It Out

Create listening activities with your children.

- Ask them: If there was one thing you could change about the world, what would it be? You might conduct the conversation while they have something to keep their hands busy, such as LEGO bricks or pens and paper. You might conduct the conversation while going on a walk or cycle around the neighborhood.

- Capture their responses together with words, pictures, and creations and continue to ask questions about them.

- Keep track of the questions and continue to explore them. You might keep a journal of questions as a family. You might create a "parking lot/car park" on your wall using newsprint, a place where family members can "park" questions as they come up. As time allows, you can then explore these questions as a family.

7

Waiting for One Another

Brian Brock

What does it look like to wait for one another in our families? And how does this practice relate to the active pursuit of a more just society?

Waiting for Adam

I pondered these questions recently while sitting in the bath with my eldest son, Adam. Adam is halfway through his seventeenth year, and the shared tub is getting a bit tight. Adam has Down syndrome, but the more relevant issue is that he is on the autism spectrum. He's non-verbal, though very communicative in his own way. We think of him as around 120 pounds of rapidly maturing body and a mental age of around three. Tub time is good time.

It's also a time to look after his body. He's at the stage of needing to shave now and then, though he doesn't realize it. When I'm shaving his chin in the bath, I wonder: How long will I be doing this? Will he ever groom himself? It was a family milestone when he decided that his tenth birthday gift to us was to sit on the toilet rather than in soiled diapers. He's never done any of this self-care on his own.

Caring for the body of another person brings to mind the enigmatic saying of Paul about husband and wife: Your body is not your own. I find myself wondering what this encourages us to recognize about our children. Paul apparently assumes that the love of man and wife tends toward the generation of additional bodies, those of children. Then, the normal course of every child's life is to move from being in the womb and hardly distinguishable from the life of the mother, to slowly being differentiated, first by being born and then, over years, becoming a fully individuated and self-aware individual. That's if things go as we expect.

Things did not go as we expected with Adam. He certainly has his own individual identity and is aware that his opinions and desires differ in important respects from ours. But his ideas about self-care are rudimentary at best. We have no choice but to care for him as if his body were our own.

This is awkward territory today. We don't like to acknowledge that a late-teen and an adult parent might bathe together, as the complexities of caregiving relationships that both require and forbid intimate touching demand attunement to the erotic level of our relationships.[44] Ours is a society focused on bringing children to independence and autonomy, to help them identify their own goals, to direct their days and ultimately their own lives. We know that hovering parents can stunt that process. It is entirely understandable that young neurodivergent adults who live with their parents (such as those on the autism spectrum) lament their parents blocking their desires to grow up and make their own choices. Knowing all this, it is equally obvious that our goal cannot be to help Adam grow into the ideal of our society—the autonomous decision maker capable of making money and being a good taxpaying consumer.

How then should I respond to the conditions that life with Adam imposes on our family life, and on my life as an academic? Today I write thoughts from yesterday's bath time, and I have no choice but to do so with Adam sitting right next to me on the couch. He's rocking so vigorously, I actively have to resist asking the question of whether I should put down the computer and take him out for a walk.

This inner work is the practice I call "waiting for Adam." This chapter attempts to hand on to you what I've learned in attempting to travel at his speed, and to invite you to try it yourself. Does slowing down to

---

[44]Cristina L. H. Traina, *Erotic Attunement: Parenthood and the Ethics of Sensuality between Unequals* (Chicago: University of Chicago Press, 2011), 141–170.

be with Adam lead me outward to care for others in similar situations, or toward an isolated and defensive crouch? How does learning to wait for Adam teach me to speak up for justice in my community? Such a practice begins in an empathetic connection that grows into an examination of my own reasons to move ahead without him that becomes transformative when I learn to recognize and prayerfully repent of my impatience. Thus, the practice of living and working with Adam calls forth an empathetic connection with all the other families in my city and region who are also feeling trapped by their caring role and abandoned by any support networks.

Everyday Caring Is a Political Act

Waiting on and caring for Adam's body are undervalued practices in economic, political, and ethical discussions in Western contexts because these are practices typically delegated to women. That I embrace significant childcare responsibilities at all marks me as an heir and product of the second wave of feminist thinking emerging from the 1970s and 1980s. Second-wave feminists pushed the question of feminism beyond the simple right of women to vote and into much broader territory about who does the dishes and who cares for children or the elderly, for example.[45]

These feminist thinkers developed a theoretical framework that allowed them to make sense of the wide range of human experiences that had been ignored in traditional patriarchal societies. As Eva Feder Kittay observes,

> Dependents, require care ... questions of who takes on the responsibility of care, who does the hands-on care, who sees to it that caring is done and done well, and who provides the support for the relationship of care and for both parties to the caring relationship—these are social and political questions...

[45]The gendering of labor in the home and workplace and its ethical implications has been richly engaged by thinkers such as: Virginia Held, *The Ethics of Care: Personal, Political, Global* (Oxford: Oxford University Press, 2003); Michael Fine, "Eva Feder Kittay: Dependency Work and the Social Division of Care," in *The Palgrave Handbook of Social Theory in Health, Illness and Medicine,* ed. F. Collyer (London: Palgrave Macmillan, 2015), 628–43; Nell Noddings, *Caring: A Feminine Approach to Ethics and Moral Education,* 2nd ed. (Berkeley: University of California Press, 2003); and Martha C. Nussbaum, *Frontiers of Justice: Disability, Nationality, Species Membership* (Cambridge, MA: Belknap Press, 2006), chaps. 2–3.

How a society organizes care of these needs is a matter of social justice.[46]

A feminist care ethic emphasizes the moral seriousness of attending to the hands-on care of children and those with disabilities *and* highlights the direct political implications of this commitment. *Waiting for Adam is not only an act of care inside the home; at the same time it is also a form of political engagement.*

Philosophers engage few of the practices that sustain domestic life in Western households. Almost to a man (and almost all of them *were* men), they never made it past occasionally exploiting disability as a grab-bag of interesting philosophical examples.[47] To make their point about the political importance of caring practices, feminist thinkers had to challenge deep-seated academic conventions, which they have done by encouraging academics to "openly acknowledge the backgrounds from which they speak so that their hearers can better understand the contexts of their experiences," as Virginia Held put it.[48] By telling my story, I show myself in a second way to be an heir of feminist intellectual work.

This shift in perspective and method has drawn attention to modes of listening and engaging emotionally with the world that modern academic philosophy and theology have often marginalized. Put more precisely, most modern moral philosophy (which has strongly shaped Christian ethical thinking) assumes a narrow form of reasoning. Ethicists of many types invite us to define good actions in conceptual terms and by rational means—to work/think our way toward what we are supposed to be and do. Our emotions, these ethicists suggest, may *motivate* us, but they do not do any *definitional* work in describing the good act or the good life. In other words, these dominant traditions in philosophical ethics insist on a separation between reason (narrowly construed) and emotion.

It is here that feminists typically cry foul. Emotional engagement with the world plays a crucial role in developing moral understanding in

[46]Eva Feder Kittay, *Love's Labor: Essays on Women, Equality, and Dependency* (New York: Routledge, 1999), 1.

[47]Licia Carlson, *The Faces of Intellectual Disability: Philosophical Reflections* (Bloomington, IN: University of Indiana Press, 2010).

[48]Virginia Held, *Feminist Morality: Transforming Culture, Society and Politics* (Chicago: University of Chicago Press, 1993), 19.

its most basic forms. We are born into a world whose moral shape first appears to us through the care we receive, and we teach others certainly through the ideas we explicitly hand on, but perhaps more broadly and profoundly through how we show them the things for which we care and that we love in the course of everyday living. Hence, observes Held,

> The emphasis of many feminists working in ethics and in moral development...on the concerns and implications of *caring*: caring for children, caring for the ill or infirm, caring about the feelings of others, and understanding how to care for human beings, including ourselves, enmeshed as we are in human relationships, and finally, also caring about the globe. The caring so central here is partly emotional. It involves feelings and requires high degrees of empathy to enable us to discern what morally recommends in our caring activities.[49]

In my case, caring for Adam has opened a whole new world of relationships to me—the world of disability. Adam's birth meant disability would never again be merely a theoretical theme at the margins of my work in theology and medical ethics. Rather, disability became a site of love, a source of knowledge, and a central place for moral reflection.

The power of love, emotional engagement, and bodily care for one another, it turns out, are also themes tightly interwoven in the New Testament.

Freed by a Foolish Cross

The apostle Paul is not often thought of as a pro-feminist thinker. Yet as the blind theologian John Hull observes, Paul's use of visual metaphors is a clue that there may be a Paul who has been overlooked by many Christians. The apostle characteristically employs visual metaphors in a much less either/or fashion than other biblical authors. In the gospel of John, for instance, people are *either* sighted or blind, nothing in between. Paul, in contrast, continually draws on images of foggy mirrors, of blurry vision, and of eyes being scaled over.[50]

---

[49]Ibid., 30.

[50]John M. Hull, *In the Beginning There Was Darkness: A Blind Person's Conversations with the Bible* (London: SCM, 2001), 84–91.

In Galatians 4:13–16 Paul also speaks of having a debilitating illness and of his gratitude to the Galatian Christians for not having treated him with the typical contempt or "scorn" (4:14) reserved for disabled people. Rather, "had it been possible, you would have torn out your eyes and given them to me" (4:15). This passage, in combination with the conclusion of Galatians where Paul points out that the proof that he is taking over from his secretary is in the "large letters I make when I am writing in my own hand!" (6:11), makes it plausible to assume that what he calls the weakness of his flesh or his thorn in the flesh might well have been poor eyesight. As the disability theologian Amos Yong points out, "Perhaps the closest ancient Greek parallel to the modern term 'disability' is the word *asthenēs* ('weak') and its correlates."[51]

It may be Paul's personal experience with disability that led him to employ themes that resonate with feminist and disability concerns. Two from his first letter to the Corinthian church are particularly significant. There, Paul weighs in on a debate among Christians in Corinth about the shape of the gospel. Some in the church think that the good news of Jesus is best displayed in Christians who look wise and speak persuasively. Others think that the essence of the gospel is displayed in those Christians who possess flashy spiritual gifts. Still others think that a true Christian looks like Paul or like Jesus himself.

Paul replies that the way of Jesus is the way of the cross. His pivotal assertion is striking and allows no caveats.

> Has not God made foolish the wisdom of the world?...we proclaim Christ crucified: a stumbling block to Jews and foolishness to Gentiles...For God's foolishness is wiser than human wisdom, and God's weakness is stronger than human strength. (1 Corinthians 1:20–25)

The debater and the rhetorician were the paragons of worldly intelligence in first-century Greco-Roman culture. By definition, people who needed care or had disabilities were their opposite, the "weak." And it is with these people that Paul identifies not only himself, but his gospel.

The term "foolishness" appears five times in 1 Corinthians 1:18–23, despite the fact that the term (literally, "moron") was as pejorative

---

[51] Amos Yong, *The Bible, Disability, and the Church: A New Vision of the People of God* (Grand Rapids, MI: Eerdmans, 2011), 84.

in Paul's time as it remains today. Yet this is precisely the site where Paul keeps insisting that the saving power of the crucified Christ will appear. Paul also emphasizes that there are different kinds of wisdom. The wisdom that most people want aspires to join the powerful and influential, the upper crust. For Paul the cross offers a counter-wisdom found among the foolish.

It is hard to imagine that Paul does not have people with all sorts of disabilities in mind, especially those with intellectual disabilities, when he summarizes his core claim in 1 Corinthians 1:27: "But God chose what is foolish in the world to shame the wise; God chose what is weak in the world to shame the strong." Beyond siding with the weak against the strong, he insists that this is the cosmic reality revealed in the work of Jesus Christ, and specifically in his work on the cross.

The crucified Christ is the supreme symbol of all that was weak and foolish in the Roman world. Famously, the earliest picture of Jesus ever found by archaeologists is a mocking cartoon of a crucified man depicted with the head of an ass.[52] Paul has been so deeply schooled in the stories of Israel that he knows that God raises his children up out of defeat. Rather than try to hide the shame of a crucified messiah, Paul draws attention to it. In our terms, the crucified person is the ultimate dis-abled person, an inhabitant of the most stigmatized social location that can be achieved in Roman society.

It is this Jesus whom Paul insists on presenting as an alternative to those Corinthian Christians' vision of a Jesus who is perfect, powerful, polished, and well-spoken. "I decided to know nothing among you except Jesus Christ, and him crucified...so that your faith might rest not on human wisdom but on the power of God" (1 Corinthians 2:2–5). In following a Christ who is most powerful in weakness, Paul discovers a new vision of how Christians are to relate to one another.

To Love Well Is to Wait Well

To care for bodies—individual and collective—is to gain ethical insight. Paul focuses his attention (and ours) on the broken body of Christ as a site of care and knowledge, of moral attention. In

---

[52]This earliest known picture of Jesus is called the Alexamenos graffito, and it was found etched in plaster in first-century Rome. "Alexamenos Graffito," *Bible Odyssey*, 2019, https://www.bibleodyssey.org/en/tools/image-gallery/a/alexamenos-graffito.

1 Corinthians 11:17–34, Paul shows us that the Christian ethical life is not entered by thinking about universal humanity, but by attending to differences, especially of those who have been located as outsiders to social capital or as untouchables.

In the first few decades of the Christian movement, churches had no purpose-built buildings in which to meet. The church gathered in the houses of its rich members, including for worship services. Rich people in the Roman world practiced all the usual conventions of elite social gatherings. They knew who was appropriate to invite to a party and how to keep appropriate distance between those who were being served and those who served them. And they were comfortable getting a little tipsy together—with the other more elite members of the community.[53]

By calling himself a follower of a humiliated, crucified Christ, Paul firmly identifies himself from the outset of the letter as allied with the bodies and the plight of the most vulnerable. The presenting issue is that the rich Corinthian Christians are having what they would consider a normal dinner party, while the poor Christians (almost all of whom were slaves) were coming in at the end after a long day and being given whatever scraps were left over from the fellowship meal that the wealthier Christians had been enjoying for some hours. To highlight how this insult injures the body of Christ, Paul calls it a humiliation of the weakest.

For Paul, such behavior makes a mockery of the foolishness of the cross, and he explodes:

> When you come together, it is not really to eat the Lord's supper. For when the time comes to eat, each of you goes ahead with your own supper, and one goes hungry and another becomes drunk. What! Do you not have homes to eat and drink in? Or do you show contempt for the church of God and humiliate those who have nothing? What should I say to you? Should I commend you? In this matter I do not commend you! (1 Corinthians 11:20–22)[54]

---

[53]The historical evidence for this claim is surveyed in Brian Brock and Bernd Wannenwetsch, *The Therapy of the Christian Body: A Theological Exposition of Paul's First Letter to the Corinthians*, vol. 2 (Eugene, OR: Cascade Books, 2018), 53–55.

[54]The disability implications of this chapter are discussed in more detail in Brock and Wannenwetsch, *Therapy of the Christian Body*, 66–71.

Paul is genuinely angry. His anger is directly linked to the theme of disability, because slavery in the ancient world (as in almost every culture) is disabling. The slave's body is to be used—and used up. What causes so much offense about the confusion of church with a rich person's meal is that it once again ignores those whose labor has made the feasting possible, the slaves in their community. The domination relations that characterize their economics are colonizing their gathering as church.

Paul indirectly highlights the connection between slavery and domination when he says in 1 Corinthians 11:30, "For this reason many of you are weak and ill, and some have died." Paul is not saying that the community is being judged (or punished) with illness because it is sinning. He is saying that the relational patterns in this church community are sick, unhealthy. Sick patterns of relationships make people sick. They rob other bodies of the strength they need to stay well. Paul is genuinely offended that a thieving form of social order has infected the church. Those who are getting fat off the labor of others in their daily economic relations do the same when they gather for the Lord's Supper.

His proposal to fix the problem in the Corinthian church is remarkably simple. It is so simple that it is tempting to dismiss it as not really serious. "So then, my brothers and sisters, when you come together to eat, *wait for one another*" (1 Corinthians 11:33, my emphasis). It's hard to believe that this could be Paul's proposed solution. Yet he really seems to mean it when he says that the power of God is shown in weakness. There is no irony in his insistence that he follows a God who became a humiliated outcast to reveal that no one is a humiliated outcast.

Paul always emphasizes having been baptized into Christ's *death,* not his resurrection, his power, or his glory.[55] We are united as Christians

---

[55]Paul reiterates that his understanding of church comes from the crucified Christ in the words that now lie at the very heart of Christian worship: "For as often as you eat this bread and drink the cup, you proclaim the Lord's *death* until he comes" (1 Cor. 11:26, my emphasis). When you take communion together, Paul insists, you are proclaiming the One who was humiliated and whose body was publicly broken. Whoever once again humiliates those whose bodies are humiliated and broken "will be answerable for the body and blood of the Lord" (11:27). Christians prove they despise weakness in the ways they act toward those they assume to be weak or socially inconsequential.

in communion in the very mode of God's reaching out to all of us through this moment of God's own brokenness. Christ is "broken and given." If you take that seriously, really seriously, Paul teaches, you will wait for one another. Those who know themselves as broken, as united in a broken Christ, never rush ahead without the others. Those who have power will know that it *must* be employed in attentive care for those without social power or other kinds of social capital. Those who know themselves in the crucified One will be looking out for and embracing people who seem to offer nothing, who appear not to be able to contribute. To do so makes them a community that is continually having to learn what it means to travel at the speed of others so that the bonds of community can flourish.[56]

The Practice of Waiting Well

As we relinquish an understanding of the good news of Jesus as an offer of power, security, and success, we Christians begin to understand our intrinsic connections with one another. Not every Christian will have a disabled child. But every family will regularly encounter invitations to slow down and wait for someone. These are often moments of tension in a family. I, for one, am tempted to say "Hurry up" to my family members, and not in the nicest tone of voice. Divisions are born in such moments that grow to become destructive of justice in communities. Getting good at waiting, at travelling at the speed of the slowest in our families, is a deep practice, one that takes a lifetime to master.

In our family, loving one another well means recognizing that we won't leave the house until Adam has his shoes on. (I wonder what it might mean for your family.) Some of us might want to charge ahead and leave others to do it for him ("I'll just wait in the car"). Others might hide out in another room until the job gets done by someone else. The one who does it will often be tempted to be rough with Adam for not being able to do it himself. I have already confessed my temptation to bark orders to get people moving. Getting out the door together requires inner work and discipleship from every family member. Every member must be constantly learning to attend better to what needs to be done if we are to stay together. Such a desire springs from

---

[56]John Swinton, *Becoming Friends of Time: Disability, Timefulness, and Gentle Discipleship* (Waco, TX: Baylor University Press, 2018), 35–53, 115–129.

an empathetic engagement with the plight of all the others and the patience to enact the care that is needed with good grace.[57] Exactly the same spiritual work is required if we are to engage repentantly and constructively in patiently bending the relationships that make our cities and nations more just.

These are practices that change our way of living in the world. In attending to how divisions form in our families, Paul teaches us, we are learning something crucial about how to combat the divisions between people and classes that make our societies so unhealthy. As I learn to wait for Adam, as I care for his body in the bathtub and elsewhere, I think about his classmates at his special school. Who looks after them? And who speaks up for their typically invisible and unpaid carers? Waiting for Adam—a child of the crucified Christ— opens in me a new empathy with the Polish single mother who cares for one of his classmates with special needs, and the Indian parents of the other boy with Down syndrome in his class. As an educated and articulate speaker, will I speak up for them in the political contexts in which the levels of their social support are decided? Or will I focus my efforts on little more than ensuring that others support me? Having been patiently but persistently loved with compassion by God, I am learning to become someone who serves that divine compassion, that empathetic slowing down modelled by Paul that concretely embodies God's love and justice.

Try It Out

Because the practical work Paul has suggested is seemingly so simple—wait for one another—the real work here lies in fostering practices of observation, reflection, and prayerful repentance and change. As you consider this chapter in your own family, you might ask these questions:

- Who in your family tries your patience? How will you have to change to love them well and travel at their speed?

---

[57]For an excellent and accessible treatment of these themes more explicitly focused on the challenges of parenting a disabled child, see Hollie M. Holt-Woehl, *They Don't Come with Instructions: Cries, Wisdom, and Hope for Parenting Children with Developmental Challenges* (Minneapolis, MN: Fortress Press, 2018).

- Who in your neighborhood tries your patience? How will you have to change to take their lives and needs seriously?

- Which voices in public debates about political issues try your patience? What inner work do you need to do to listen to them and hear their needs as people for whom Christ also died?

8

Pilgrimage of Solidarity

Anton Flores-Maisonet

I met my brother on the streets of Mexico City.

As a member of the elite Atlanta Boy Choir on tour in Mexico, I was standing outside a restaurant with the others when a little boy saw past our fancy wool blazers and clip-on ties and approached us, his jeans filthy and his shirt white only in memory.

In my meager Spanish I asked the little boy his name.

"Alejandro," he replied.

To my question of how old he was, he replied, "*Tengo siete años.*"

I saw more than just a seven-year-old boy abandoned to the streets by a society built on inequality, and I felt more than just compassion: I had a mystical encounter. Back home I had a younger brother awaiting my return to America's comfortable suburbs. My brother's name? Alejandro. Aged seven.

My conversation with my brother-on-the-streets ended abruptly when one of the choir's chaperones shooed Alejandro away and then proceeded to reprimand me for engaging in such "reckless" behavior.

My life's mantra is "Love crosses borders." I have traveled to faraway lands such as Colombia and Palestine to witness and join the reckless work of reconciliation in a world filled with conflict and division. I've been arrested (even with my children present) in my own country for acts deemed civil disobedience that I understand as divine obedience. My family and I have lived in an intentional community with migrants, and I co-founded Casa Alterna, which offers hospitality, accompaniment, and assistance at no cost to individuals and families fighting for asylum and against deportation. I'm not immune to fear, but I'm more afraid of what it means to my children and their future if I don't live with integrity and in alignment with my deepest ideals and values.

This chapter explores what it means to raise children whose "reckless" behavior moves them deeper into solidarity with the challenges of their lifetime. We know there's a widening chasm between the haves and have-nots. We know that globalization is shrinking our planet and that the climate change resulting from that globalization threatens to make it uninhabitable. We know that politicians want us to believe that systemic racism is a figment of our imaginations, yet racialized mass incarceration persists and police brutality doesn't escape the livestream of a bystander's phone. We push the poor in the Two-Thirds World off their lands, and when they migrate to our borders we exploit them for cheap labor—and then deport them via prisons of profit. And then we gaze at our children and have to decide: Do we try to shield them from the harsh complexities of social injustice? Or do we equip them for radical change? This book and this chapter is for you who seek the latter.

The good news is that you are not alone. There are guideposts along this journey, and this chapter shares a few that I have found in the book of Exodus. The exodus story is a long journey of liberation, one in which Pharaoh becomes smaller and smaller in the rearview mirror and Yahweh becomes more prominent.[58] It's a perfect case study for how systems of domination rewrite history and use fear-based rhetoric and harsh policies to increase their power. But the journey is also a time in which we see the birth pangs of liberation coming from

[58]Walter Brueggemann, "Exodus Teaching," YouTube video, 35:08, posted by Episcopal Diocese of Southern Ohio, August 29, 2017, https://youtu.be/_mMZ-i3t1rzw.

below. We witness low-status women engage in the first recorded act of civil disobedience in the Hebrew text, their names, Shiphrah and Puah, preserved throughout history. And we see Moses learn the hard lessons of counterviolence, flee in fear, and be awakened and called back to the place of his worst act as a leader of a liberatory social movement. Moses was called from the burning bush: "And Yahweh said, 'Surely I have seen the misery of my people who *are* in Egypt, and I have heard their cry of distress because of their oppressors, for I know their sufferings'" (Exodus 3:7, LEB). This statement reshaped how I view the developmental process of becoming God's human agent of redemptive solidarity and how I have learned to shape the values and habits of my children.

Look at the verbs: Yahweh *sees*. Yahweh *hears*. Yahweh *knows*.

How might we help our children to *see* the world as God does, to *hear* the voices of the voiceless that God hears, and to *know* what it means to lead a compassionate life of radical solidarity for planetary justice? Staying anchored to these verbs and their calling, I explore practices that nurture within our children a sympathy that is wide-eyed, an empathy borne of deep listening, and a compassionate heart that engages in radical, reckless solidarity with those on the margins of our fragmented world.

Time to take off our sandals and invite God to turn this time of reading and reflection into holy ground!

Helping Our Children to See as God Sees

And Yahweh said, "Surely I have seen the misery of my people who are in Egypt" (Exodus 3:7, LEB).

One day I accompanied "Felipa" to the Atlanta airport. Felipa was a migrant who had fled both national and domestic violence. As an asylum seeker in the United States, Felipa promised her two children she would do all she could to reunite them in a new land one day. The children moved in with their maternal grandparents, and Felipa worked hard to keep her promise. One at a time, Felipa's children reunited with their mother in the United States.

On this day, after two years of separation, it was the turn of her now teenaged daughter "Griselda." The reunion was emotional; tears of joy intermingled with fast-flowing Spanish words of endearment and the tender embrace of mother and daughter separated too long.

As we got into my car, Felipa was anxious to point out places of interest in this new land so different from the mountain highlands that Griselda knew as home. But Felipa's enthusiasm found competition: Cell phones and social media had not bypassed Griselda's rural community, and she escaped into her mother's cell phone and connected with friends far away but within virtual grasp.

Isn't that every parent's struggle? We long to see our children fully present to the physical world around them. How much more challenging it is to help our children see the spiritual dimensions of realities that are often hidden in plain sight: structural violence, inequality, oppression, and repression.

To help our children see the world as God sees it, we need to be intentional. Culture is a powerful force. It is a lens by which we interpret our social interactions and find meaning. Culture also orients us to all the ways our values and roles in society are antithetical to the reign of God. If you're in the US, your child likely recites the Pledge of Allegiance daily at school without really understanding what a pledge is, much less allegiance to the symbol of a government whose people not only claim virtues such as democracy and family but also cling to poisonous myths such as white supremacy, patriarchy, and unbridled capitalism. To raise a child who can see beyond such culturally prescribed blinders means parenting with a great deal of intentionality.

To help our children see the world as God sees it also requires tenacious courage. As biblical scholar Walter Brueggemann writes, "Exodus is the tale of Moses' courageous life lived in defiance of Pharaoh for the sake of God's liberating resolve. Indeed, the resolve of God would not amount to much without the risky courage of Moses."[59] To cultivate prophetic courage in our children, we help them to confront their fears, especially those conditioned by society. Recall what you have already done to develop your child's healthy risk taking: Stood in a pool and encouraged your child to trust your arms more than the deep waters around you? Tucked a note of encouragement

---

[59]Walter Brueggemann and Charles L. Campbell, *The Threat of Life: Sessions on Pain, Power, and Weakness* (Minneapolis, MN: Fortress Press, 1996), 22.

in their backpack on their frightful first day of school? Parental love is foundational for a child's sense of trust and security. It's what reminds them as they move toward greater independence that there is a love and a freedom greater than their fears. Oh, how I wish the boy's choir chaperone had joined my conversation with young Alejandro rather than shooing him away!

With these foundational disciplines of intentionality and courage, families can practice seeing as God sees. When our two boys, Eli and Jairo, were smaller, my wife, Charlotte, and I loved taking them geocaching, a global game of hide-and-seek in which fellow enthusiasts hide containers in plain sight and find others via GPS coordinates. Below are some spiritual coordinates for what I call *theocaching*— tapping into unseen spiritual guides to find what has always been hidden in plain sight.

After adopting our eldest son from Guatemala, we began to attend a Spanish-language church. Our intent was simply to keep Jairo connected to other Guatemalans, but God had greater plans. God used this time of worshipping alongside mostly poor, unauthorizable[60] immigrants to open our eyes to the incessant challenges that confront those who live in our country without means of obtaining legal status. Yet we also witnessed a dignified faith amongst strangers who called us their siblings (*hermanos* and *hermanas*).

One Christmas our youngest son, Eli, requested a map of the world and some push pins. He hung the map on his bedroom wall, and every time we welcomed a guest into our home (and that was quite often), Eli would escort the guest into his bedroom and invite them to pin their place of birth on the map. Over time, the map became a mosaic chronicling all who had entered our home and Eli's unique gift of welcoming the stranger. Through intentional and "reckless" practices of relationship-building, our family has practiced seeing as God sees: seeing siblings rather than strangers.

At Christmas time, we limited our boys to three modest gifts from the Magi. When we came home from our consumption feasts with extended family, before all their new toys could go in their room, they had to

---

[60]This is a word of my own creation. When speaking of immigrants without legal status, I often change the -ed suffix to -able (i.e., unlicensed or unauthorized to unlicenseable or unauthorizable). In my view, this shifts the conversation from "Why don't they get authorized?" to "Why can't they get authorized?"

remove an equal number of old toys that we'd then donate. Because we did this from an early age, it became just another joy-filled tradition that reinforced our value of simplicity. Another simple way we practiced presence with ourselves and one another was "Unplugged Sundays." (Our oldest son didn't like this experiment at all.)

Yet another practice has been to choose to eat in the homes of immigrant entrepreneurs who run off-the-grid restaurants. This helped our boys see a hidden reality of our world. What hidden gems in how the "other half lives"[61] can you discover with your children?

We spent three full summers in Guatemala, enrolling our monolingual boys in pre-school and public school there as a way to immerse them in a completely different experience. Where do your kids spend their summers? Where and what do they learn in both formal and informal settings? What intentional shifts might you engineer to make space for eye-opening encounters?

Your experiments don't have to be grandiose, just intentional. Get your books from the public library instead of online. Take your children to a public laundromat and teach them to wash their clothes there. Take public transportation together. Play at a park or swim in a pool where you and your children are the outsiders.

I have come to think of these practices as akin to Gandhi's language for his autobiographical journey: "my experiments with truth." Alongside our children, we have tried to make our lives an experiment with the truth of our highest ideals in hopes they'll see life through a more truthful lens. Through experiments and theocaching, we are all learning to see as God sees.

Helping Our Children Hear the Voices of the Voiceless

And Yahweh said, "I have heard their cry of distress because of their oppressors" (Exodus 3:7, LEB).

I met "Paola" in our local jail. She was facing two years in prison and then a likely deportation to her home country. Her two US-born children had already been repatriated to the place of their mother's birth, but Paola was pregnant and would give birth to her third child while incarcerated.

---

[61]Jacob A. Riis, *How the Other Half Lives: Studies among the Tenements of New York* (Eastford, CT: Martino Publishing, 2015.)

During a chaplaincy visit with Paola, she asked me the unexpected. "Would you care for my baby when it's born?"

"Why me?" I asked, since she had many close friends who would gladly care for her yet unborn child.

"Because you're the only US citizen I know and trust, and I want my child returned to me if I'm deported."

We did welcome baby Emanuel ("God-with-us") into our home and hearts. Charlotte and I called him "Manny"; our boys called him "Little Man." Together we shared a journey of fostering a child and hearing the cries of the voiceless (especially in the wee hours of the night).

When it came time for Manny to join his family in Central America, I penned a song for our family that ended:

> *Immanuel, Immanuel,*
>
> *God with us, can make us well;*
>
> *In this ol' world so filled with fear,*
>
> *O draw us close, please draw us near.*

> *As we prepare to say goodbye,*
>
> *Jesus, hold this child nigh;*
>
> *You're God with us, be God with him;*
>
> *Immanuel, be God with him.*

Jairo was already a young teen when Manny lived with us. Upon Manny's departure, he took to social media, posted photos he had taken of Manny over the months, and wrote, "After a long fifteen months for caring for this child, today is finally the day. He has really made a huge impact on my life. Goodbye, Little Man." Our relationship with Manny helped our children to hear the voice of the voiceless and helped our whole family to practice theological reflection together.

It's important to reflect and process the pains of the world theologically with our children because the pains are great. Secondary trauma is real, and systemic oppression is complex. Listening to how our children integrate these experiences into their worldview can help them to hear themselves as they live into a new perspective. Without judgment, ask open-ended questions, reflect back what you hear, and empathize with what your child is feeling. Our youngest son, Eli, often processed his feelings about human suffering through powerful poetry, such as this one:

TRAIL OF TEARS

Gone are the mountains,

Gone are the trees.

To the west we must go,

Not stopping to lament our woes.

Our home is far, so far.

Gone are the wails of ancestors.

They told us to take

What was on our backs.

Then the White Man takes

More than they need.

Our land, our heritage,

Crushed beneath their shiny, black boots.

The trail we walk,

The tears we shed.

Death all around,

Feet freezing cold in gray snow.

What more must we suffer

On this solemn Trail of Tears?

Manny's departure was more than just the day we bid farewell to God-with-us in the form of a child: That day our entire family, including our children, bid farewell to the privilege of being muted to the harsh realities of this world and open to how God speaks to us through the disempowered and vulnerable in society. No longer is mass incarceration, immigration detention, or foster care hidden in plain sight. It has a voice and a name: God-with-us. Through family reflection interwoven with theological reflection, we can help deepen our children's capacities to hear with new ears, ears more attuned to God's voice. My song, Jairo's post, and Eli's poem represent the ways we gave voice to the presence of a God-who-is-with-us-all.

Helping Your Children Form Hearts of Compassion

And Yahweh said, "I know their sufferings" (Exodus 3:7, LEB).

The Hebrew word for "know" here in Exodus 3:7 is עָדַיְ(yā·da').[62] Rather than being restricted to the intellect and mental activity, such knowledge draws from the emotions and from experience, and may encompass such qualities as contact, intimacy, concern, relatedness, and mutuality.

Juxtapose this experiential, emotional knowledge to that of Pharaoh who *"did not know* Joseph" (Exodus 1:8, LEB, emphasis mine). Such disregard and dehumanization exacerbate violence and injustice in the world today. Our children need knowledge that comes from the head and the heart, one where empathy and solidarity open our eyes and ears from blinding and deafening privilege. Fostering in our kids a heart that knows the sufferings of others could be the single most revolutionary thing you do as a parent.

Artie is a nurse. His younger brother, Gabriel, is attending college and also seeks a vocation in the medical field. How did two brothers, whose parents never attended college but lived in the shadows of America as hard-working immigrants without legal status, get called into similar fields and become so educated? Artie and Gabriel's mom, Norma, went into complete renal failure the day she gave birth to Gabriel. For the next fourteen years until her premature death, Artie and Gabriel served as their mom's medical interpreter and home health aide.

For all fourteen of those years, our two families lived interdependently, eventually forming an intentional community that widened each of our circles of love and support. But for Artie and Gabriel, knowing that their mother's love and aspirations for them was greater than death, and being encircled by a loving community, helped build the resilience

[62]"Bible Hub," Online Parable Bible Project, accessed November 18, 2021, http://concordances.org/hebrew/yada_3045.htm.

necessary first to bear the sight of their terminally ill mother's misery and then to rise from the ashes of grief with hearts transformed by compassion.

While we hope none of our children ever has to endure such a loss, the compassionate life is one that touches the wounds of others. A child who has been informed by a life of empathy can practice the holy gift of compassion. How can our children become compassionate caregivers and touch the wounds of a broken world? One way we do this is to help children and young people listen deeply to difficult truths and then follow their idealism as they respond.

One summer, our organization, Casa Alterna, hosted a Freedom School for first-wave Latinx immigrant children who all lived in the same cul-de-sac. Together we learned about the Creek nation that first inhabited the land the children now call home and how in the early nineteenth century, the Creek were brutally removed from this land— their land—by a series of wars and lopsided treaties imposed upon them by President Andrew Jackson and the expansionist government of the United States. Then we learned about Goose Holler, the tiny enclave of Black domestic workers who also once lived in this cul-de-sac. We visited Ms. Mattie, an octogenarian Black woman who grew up in Goose Holler. She recounted what it was like during the Jim Crow era—how trash would pile up at the end of the cul-de-sac due to the city's neglect, and how she was prohibited from studying in the nearby white schools but how her daughter became one of the first to integrate those same schools. The children learned about the arsonists who burned down Welcome Baptist Church, once a vibrant place of worship for Black neighbors of Goose Holler and to this day a vacant lot.

The children had a deep awakening and wanted to act. With the assistance of a local minister, three of the oldest kids crafted a speech and delivered it before the city council. With Ms. Mattie in the audience, the children (and the children only) made a passionate plea for the formal recognition of Goose Holler. The council agreed unanimously. Because of their advocacy, the street now has a historical marker recovering the name of Goose Holler, and that vacant lot has been transformed into a pocket park called Welcome Park. When children are given the freedom to follow their hearts, beauty and redemption flourish.

Let Our Children Go!

And Yahweh said, "...I have come down to deliver them from the hand of the Egyptians and to bring them up from this land to a good and wide land, to a land flowing with milk and honey..." (Exodus 3:8, LEB).

The ultimate point of raising children with God's eyes, ears, and a heart for justice is the liberation of all, oppressed *and* oppressor. As we see in Exodus, liberation involves both Israel (the oppressed) and Pharaoh (the oppressor), whether they want it or not. Liberation can be disruptive and, at times, even unwelcomed not only by the perpetrators of injustice but also by the victims. But undoing the systems of violence and suffering is God's endgame.[63] As parents and nurturers our task is to help children face these hard truths in developmentally appropriate ways, to help them place Christ at the center of their lives, and to equip them to be human agents of God's justice and redemption in everyday life.

Now is the time to cultivate a spirit of courage and resistance within our children. Egypt is crumbling and the liberation of all our children will not be found within it. There is a good and wide land with enough for everyone. Let's raise our children so that it will be their generation that sees "the resurrection of all flesh and the renewal of heaven and earth,"[64] for that is the destination of the timeless Exodus journey.

Try It Out

While there is no single way to embark on this downward journey toward solidarity and mutual liberation, there are many intentional steps a family can make toward the promised land of beloved community. Consider planning a reverse pilgrimage with your child. A reverse pilgrimage is an opportunity to see oneself in the reflection of a new mirror, an opportunity to pause from the rat race and embrace one's own complicity and powerlessness in the face of massive inequality. It can happen in your own community or halfway

---

[63]Stephanie Price, "Exodus Sermon Series: Where We Started," *The Land*, accessed August 4, 2020, https://thelandaurora.org/exodus-sermon-series-where-we-started/.

[64]Leonardo Boff, *Judaism, Christianity, and Liberation: An Agenda for Dialogue*, Otto Maduro, ed. (Eugene, OR: Wipf & Stock, 2008), 23–32.

across the world. The intention of the journey matters more than the destination. Reverse pilgrimage is a journey inward through which we—we hope—are the ones being changed.

- Don't serve behind the counter of a soup kitchen: Visit a soup kitchen, stand in line, be fed, and sit down at the table with your children and the unhoused. Introduce yourselves and ask their names. Shake your companions' hands. And then listen. Listen deeply.

- Ask good open-ended questions, and don't forget to share about yourselves as well. Don't just probe their sorrows, but don't be afraid of that either.

- Establish common ground. Get your children to ask your new companion(s) about their childhood. What common interests did (or do) they share?

- When the meal is over, give your sincere gratitude and maybe an embrace.

- On the journey home, explore with your child what this reverse pilgrimage meant to them, using these questions:

  — What did your eyes see that inspired or confused you today? How do you think God saw that?

  — What is something our meal companion shared that most affected you?

  — What do you think breaks the heart of God in what we experienced today? What of what we experienced today fills God's heart with love?

  — Now what is God inviting us to do in response?

9

Street Protesting and Self-Esteem

Leah Gunning Francis

George Floyd's tragic death in Minneapolis sparked a wave of protests across the US. In Indianapolis, we at Faith In Indiana (FII)—a local organization that brings together faith communities to work together for racial and economic justice—organized a protest against the police violence that took George Floyd's life and that of too many other unarmed Black people. More than a thousand people joined the protest, rallying at the Indiana Statehouse in Indianapolis and marching to the city-county building. Prayers, songs, and impassioned speeches that included our list of demands for anti-racist policing were all part of our protest. And so were our two children and those of many other parents.

This essay addresses the practice of street protesting with children. For my own African American family, this practice is embedded in the larger context of addressing racial injustice, while at the same time building the self-esteem of our Black children. I explore some of the issues related to raising Black children in the United States, identify from where I draw inspiration and how I strengthen my resolve, and address the efficacy of street protesting as a viable way for children to become agents of the social transformation we wish to see. Though our children did not create the problem of racism, through such protest we are empowering them to address it, while also attending to their need for an enjoyable childhood.

Raising Black Sons in the US

For nine minutes and twenty-nine seconds, George Floyd lay handcuffed and pinned beneath a police officer's knee on Chicago Avenue in Minneapolis. Bystanders including teenagers, a young child, middle-aged people, and an off-duty firefighter who happened upon this horrific scene bravely spoke up and tried to convince the officer to get off Floyd's neck. They had to balance talking cautiously to the officer with risking arrest or worse for alleged "obstruction of justice." All of their measured efforts were to no avail. A nearby high school student, accompanied by her nine-year-old cousin, video-recorded what became the last minutes of Floyd's life. This child's video, which has been shown around the world, captured the pleas of Floyd as he begged the officer to get off of him. "Please Man!" he gasped, but to no avail. With his final breaths, he called out for his deceased mother: "Momma. Momma...I'm through." Soon after, he closed his eyes for the last time.

I am the mother of two African American teenage boys. We now live in an era in which Black boys go from being perceived as "cute little boys" to "looking older than they are." In 2014, when twelve-year-old Tamir Rice was shot and killed on a Cleveland-area playground while standing alone and holding a toy gun, the officers insisted they had believed him to be much older than twelve. How they determined that in the two seconds it took them to drive onto the scene and shoot him they have yet to explain. Black children lose their perception of "innocence" before white children, leaving them susceptible to and vulnerable to any police officer, teacher, or Neighborhood Watch person who might happen to view them through the lens of racial bias.

Even though my sons' voices have deepened slightly and their legs have grown longer, any reasonable person would still regard them as young teenagers. However, the US' status as a world leader in COVID-19 infections and deaths reminds us that "reasonable" judgment is not our collective default mode. This fact, coupled with the longstanding history of racism, means that my husband and I live in a perpetual state of vigilant protectiveness.

Can you imagine what it is like to live "on guard" with your sons all of the time? When we're walking down our street, we're on guard lest someone call the police because they don't think we "belong" there. When we're shopping in the local grocery store, we're on guard lest someone assume our sons are there to shoplift. When we're driving and see a police car, we're on guard lest we're stopped and made to get out of our car. "Don't run down the street." "Never leave a store without your items in a bag and your receipt in your pocket." "No, you cannot ride in a car with two other teens": the seeming ubiquitous presence of racial injustice in the midst of our everyday, ordinary lives reinforces and justifies the long list of our commands to our sons that weigh so heavy on our hearts and minds.

As Black parents, not only do we have to work overtime to keep our kids safe, but we have to balance this effort with the need for them still to have vibrant and enjoyable childhoods. Children should not have to bear the burdensome responsibility of the problems that adults create. However, Black children and youth are not given a pass from the devastating effects of racism just because they are minors. This reality has long been an integral part of US history, from Black babies being taken from their parents at slave auction blocks to Black children being hit and spat upon as they tried to enter desegregated schools to being disproportionately suspended or expelled from school nowadays. Moreover, they are disproportionately arrested and incarcerated, and this process too often begins in the place they are supposed to be valued and safe—in school. For Black children and youth are disproportionately represented in juvenile justice systems across the country. For them to have a viable chance to flourish, breaking the school-to-prison pipeline is likewise essential.

As schools remain a battleground for the thriving of Black children because of our troublesome public school funding system that privileges wealthy districts and penalizes poor ones, the pervasive narrative that renders Black people as less intelligent than white people, and the prevalence of police in predominately Black schools, too many Black parents and communities are left to figure out a viable path forward in the face of these almost insurmountable odds.

To be clear, my social location and experience as a Black parent is not universal. My husband and I are fortunate to parent our sons under circumstances that permit them to have access to well-funded schools, healthy foods, adequate healthcare, and a vast array of recreational activities that are beyond the reach of many Black children because of the multigenerational impact of systemic racism. As a result, some of the issues I previously mentioned are not necessarily directly related to our sons. However, even though our boys are being raised by parents with three advanced degrees between them and have ease of access to the aforementioned opportunities, none of this protects them: not from being perceived as "intellectually inferior" by teachers, or as "up to no good" by store personnel when they're just walking around a store and looking at the items, or as being "in the wrong place" by passersby who don't believe that Black people live in that neighborhood and they must be getting ready to rob someone's house or steal a car, or as "older than they look" by police who decide to stop and interrogate them for no legitimate reason. My role as a seminary dean and my husband's clergy credentials provide no cover for our sons when they are going about their daily business without us. We send them out into the world each day with the prayer that the racialized imagination of the people they encounter will not damage their sense of self, at best, or cause irreparable harm, at worst. We have to make the most of the time at home to prepare them spiritually, emotionally, and intellectually for a world that will not always see and treat them as human beings created in the image of God, but as a racist stereotype that is intent on doing harm. And we have to do this on top of dealing with everyday issues such as the back and forth over screen time, completing homework, navigating teenage friendships and hormonal changes and all that they bring—just to name a few. This is the context in which we live but also the one in which we live out our faith.

Young, Gifted, and Black

As a family, we have always sought to integrate our life of faith with our life in the world. We try not to separate the sacred and secular in an artificial, legalistic way. God's spirit is in us, around us, outside us, and between us, and wherever we find love, justice, or joy, there is a good chance that we will find God. Therefore, we have tried to find a way to provide possibilities for our children to go against the grain of the artificial sacred/secular split and see God in unconventional places.

One of those unconventional places has been in street protests against racial injustice. Though racism is not a problem that our children created, they have to live with the potentially damaging effects of it—even as children. We believe that God is always present in the pursuit of justice. The book of Micah reminds us "to do justice, and to love kindness, and to walk humbly" with God (Micah 6:8). For our family, street protesting is not only a political act, it is a part of our religious expression. The very act of seeking to do justice is doing the work of God. We impress this upon the hearts and minds of our children so that they, too, make the explicit connection between the "doing" of justice as an essential ingredient for the life of faith.

It has been important for my husband and me to ground our children in a theological understanding of God that is consistent with scripture and connected to the reality in which they live. As Christians who believe in the life, death, and resurrection of Jesus, we have consistently exposed them to images of Jesus that are more congruent with the context in which he lived. Yes, there is a picture of a dark-skinned Jesus hanging in our home. A depiction of the Last Supper that includes dark-skinned Jesus and disciples hangs in our dining room. These portraits, along with a plethora of art in various genres by Black artists, provide a visual representation of our faith and world that often contradicts what they see in most churches, books, and public spaces. For our sons, seeing themselves in the Divine is essential to their believing they are children of God created in God's image and likeness, especially in a society that was formed and prospers by dehumanizing people who look like them.

Building self-esteem and cultivating self-love among African American children in our society is not a new endeavor. Throughout history, Black parents, teachers, pastors, and artists (among many others) have worked diligently to try to shield and strengthen the spirits of our vulnerable young. In 1964, famed playwright Lorraine Hansberry visited a group of Black students who had won a national writing contest. She commended their work and encouraged them to keep pursuing their writing with vigor and purpose:

> I wanted to be able to come here and speak with you on this occasion because you are young, gifted and Black. In the year 1964, I, for one, can think of no more dynamic combination

that a person might be. Look at the work that awaits you. Write about the world. Write about the world as it is, and as you think it ought to be and must be. Work hard at it. Care about it. Write about our people. Tell their story.[65]

Hansberry's explicit exhortation was clearly intended to inspire the students to take pride in their ethnicity and to engage their writing boldly as a vehicle to critique the status quo and help create the world they want to see. She charged them to tell the stories of a people whose truth has repeatedly been whitewashed throughout history.

In 1969, acclaimed musician Nina Simone set Hansberry's sentiments to music in her song, "Young, Gifted and Black."[66] Because both of our sons are musicians, I love to be able to expose them to positive songs that affirm their humanity and build self-esteem. This is a necessary counter to the negative stereotyping about Black youth that comes across too many airwaves and screens. Songs such as "To Be Young, Gifted and Black" are a soothing balm to the weary soul at a time when Black lives do not matter in the same way as white lives and when Black children are not afforded the luxury of merely being seen as *children*. To see themselves as young, gifted, and Black is to see themselves as full human beings created in the image of God, and not as the prescribed stereotypes promulgated by racist ideologies.

Taking It to the Streets

My husband and I are raising two African American teenage boys whom racist society regards as "problems" rather than as boys born into a racially unjust society that creates a lot of problems *for them*. Although we have a modestly affluent level of social status, they are not inoculated from the seen and unseen dangers of racism in America. Raising Black boys in the United States of America is a tricky and risky business. As we help to fashion our sons' sense of self in a healthy and life-affirming way, we want them to see themselves as agents of their own liberation and that of those who look like them. We talk honestly (in age-appropriate ways) about the realities of racism in our society

[65]American Masters, *Lorraine Hansberry: Sighted Eyes/Feeling Heart*, 2:41, directed by Tracy Heather Strain, PBS, January 19, 2018, www.pbs.org/wnet/american-masters/lorraine-hansberry-sighted-eyesfeeling-heart-documentary/9846/.

[66]Nina Simone and Weldon Irvine, "To Be Young, Gifted and Black," track 7 on *Black Gold*, RCA Victor, 1969, CD, https://genius.com/Nina-simone-to-be-young-gifted-and-black-lyrics.

while affirming their humanity as young, gifted, and Black teens. We want them to see the giftedness they have right now as adequate for speaking out against racial injustice, and we have made street activism, or protesting, a family affair.

During the protest in Indianapolis, our youngest son played the djembe drum during the rally at the statehouse. Our oldest son stood near me on the statehouse steps, clapping whenever inspired by the fiery speakers. Our family marched together to the city-county building, along with many other families, and stood in support of a more racially just and equitable world. This event was a meaningful way for our sons to engage in a tangible act of resistance against racial injustice and cultivate a sense of pride in their own ability to try and effect change.

This protest had a positive impact on our family in at least three ways: First, it gave us an opportunity to have a thoughtful conversation about why we were doing this. We engaged our sons and made space for them to share their feelings and any concerns. It was heart wrenching to hear their fear about being treated as George Floyd was, but as parents we need to hear these concerns and try and allay them in as honest a way as possible. Second, our sons were able to *see* other people who also understood this work as essential to their faith. They heard the prayers; they sang the songs; they saw the clergy collars. All of that matters for young minds that are trying to make sense of the world they inhabit. One expects to see these things in church, but the powerful impact of seeing them in the unexpected place of a street protest will remain with them forever. Third and finally, I saw the glimmer in their eyes as they applauded an inspiring speaker, marched along the route, and chanted the protest slogans. They knew they were active participants in the work of doing justice. My hope is that they carry this sense of knowing throughout their lives.

For Such a Time as This

As I reflect on the experience of protesting with and parenting "young, gifted, and Black" sons in a society that remains committed to maintaining a system of racial injustice, I have drawn inspiration and strength from the courage of Queen Esther. In the complicated biblical story of Esther's context and journey, she was raised by her uncle Mordecai after her parents died. When King Xerxes was in search of a new queen, Esther was one of the young girls brought to the palace. Her uncle Mordecai instructed her not to disclose her Jewish nationality, and she held this secret until it became clear that to remain silent would mean death for her people.

Esther eventually became the queen. When Mordecai learned of the plan of Haman, the highest official in King Xerxes' administration, to kill all of the Jews, he implored Esther to use her royal position to save her people. Esther pushed back and told Mordecai that for her to approach the king without being invited to do so would be punishable by death. Mordecai challenged her:

> "Do not think that in the king's palace you will escape any more than all the other Jews. For if you keep silence at such a time as this, relief and deliverance will rise for the Jews from another quarter, but you and your father's family will perish. Who knows? Perhaps you have come to royal dignity for just such a time as this." (Esther 4:13–14)

Mordecai made clear to Esther that her royal position could not protect her from Haman's annihilation plan. Even though she would have to break the "law" and risk death to talk to the king about sparing her people, Esther knew that she had no other real choice. Esther asked the community of Jews to fast for her for three days and concluded, "'After that I will go to the king, though it is against the law; and if I perish, I perish'" (Esther 4:16b).

It is tempting for those of us who do not feel as though we are in any type of imminent danger to dissociate ourselves from those who are. Although Esther's status as a queen created a significant social distance between her and the Jews in Susa, her uncle Mordecai helped her to understand that her ethnicity would trump her social status at the drop of a dime. Esther likely saw herself as a queen first, and only then a Jew, but her awakening shifted her thinking to see herself as a Jew with some distinct advantages of being a queen. She was still very vulnerable, but she also had access and opportunities that other Jews didn't have. Now was the time to act!

Esther's story reminds me that engaging in acts of justice is risky business. In other words, we put something on the line when we decide to speak up, stand up, or step outside of the status quo for the sake of justice. Sometimes we risk relationships with those who hold opposing views. Other times we risk our sense of physical and emotional safety, even in a nonviolent protest. In whatever way we find ourselves taking up the mantle of justice, risk is involved.

For the act of street protesting, I draw strength and courage from Esther's story. I, too, realize that the stakes are too high for me to sit on the sidelines and pretend that it is not my problem. Like Esther, we, too, are called to leverage the resources that we have to create a more just and equitable world. And our children must be part of it. Street protesting provides an opportunity to do something tangible that can create an opportunity for them to feel pride in their own actions and have a strong sense of why they are doing it.

Try It Out

Street activism, or protesting, can be a family affair for you, too. Children are often remarkably attuned to injustices in our society. Engaging them in age-appropriate ways in tangible acts of resistance such as protesting can create an invaluable opportunity for value sharing, forming identity, and cultivating empathy. Most protests in our countries are nonviolent. Why not search for organizations in your area that are *already* doing work on issues that you care about and learn more about how they engage street activism as part of their resistance efforts?

Why not talk with your children and find out what concerns them? They may have ideas of their own about a social injustice and would like to be part of the solution.

If you decide to join a protest march, consider the following:

- Decide on your *why.* What is the issue at hand, and why is it important to you? Talk with your children about your *why,* and listen intently to their own concerns related to this issue or others.

- Find out about the plan for the protest march (date, time, place, distance) and share this with your children.

- Have them make colorful signs to carry that portray the world they want to see.

- Wear comfortable sneaker-style shoes and carry a small backpack with water and snacks if needed.

- Although injustice is a serious matter, let your children know that it is okay to smile and enjoy being part of a movement for justice. Let them be themselves.

- Share your activities with other parents. You never know whom you might inspire!

10

Mourning and Imagination

Melissa Pagán

In January 2017, I took my daughter—at eleven, the eldest of my three children—to the Women's March in Los Angeles, California. The march was part of a global lament and protest to draw attention to and resist a variety of types of violence—racism, sexism, tribalism, and more—exhibited particularly in the US by newly inaugurated President Trump and his administration.

Marching with my daughter was exhilarating. She chanted, sang, and raised her fist in the air alongside 100,000+ people in Los Angeles. It was formative for her. While I have attended large-scale protests and have taken my children to some, it was the first time I had taken a child of mine to a protest so large and emotionally charged.

I tend not to take my children to larger protests as they can be taxing on both the body and the mind. For one of my sons, the crowds and noise would be disorienting because, though mild, he is on the autism spectrum. In addition, there's a safety concern: While most protesters are peaceful and respectful of children at marches, some protesters, anti-protesters, and police might deem violence to be appropriate and necessary. Further, for parents who are toting car seats, strollers, diapers, and snacks, being away from home for several hours can be difficult! And, let's face it, at a march, we want our children to be able to...march. Toddlers, well, they *toddle,* and often wherever they want! So I left my two younger children with a sitter so I could march with my daughter.

The experience with my daughter that day was indeed extraordinary, but it was built upon the *ordinary, everyday messages* related to social justice that my children commonly receive in my household. We parents know that children thrive through having structure and consistency in their lives. The things to which we expose them on a regular basis are likely to shape not only their moral character but also how and what they interpret as having meaning and moral value.

In the society we share, violence is all around us. Social media makes it more likely that we will see or hear about racism, sexism, heterosexism, and/or extra-judicial state violence. Yet such constant exposure to the ubiquity of violence tends to numb us to it instead of prompting us to act. Using the concept of *spirit murder,* this chapter addresses the challenge of numbness and describes a conversational, everyday practice for fostering intimacy through mourning and imagination.

Spirit Murder

Black feminists from the United States have claimed that violence leading to numbing is tantamount to "spirit murder," a reality in which "wounds are left on the flesh, psyche, and even soul of those who experience violence *and* the wounds...that haunt perpetrators of violence, including a willingness to accept, and to render *unseen,* those who are dispossessed."[67] The human spirit is in danger of slowly succumbing to "numbing pathologies."[68] They disrupt our moral sensibilities, narrow who we consider to be a part of our moral community of accountability, and disregard the humanity of others all while also diminishing our own humanity.

The implications of this collective spiritual death within society are many. Here, I highlight one and suggest a practice that can help us respond to it.

---

[67]Jennifer Nash, *Black Feminism Reimagined After Intersectionality* (Durham, NC: Duke University Press, 2019), 123–24.
[68]Ibid.,124.

One serious implication of spirit murder is that we become so alienated from one another that we pre-determine the lives of the vulnerable as unmournable, as lives that lack "grievability"—a term I take from theorist Judith Butler.[69] Some lives are so valued that to imagine violence being done to them would be an abomination. Yet when violence—even to death—is enacted against others' lives, it is barely even recognized. The inequality of these very different attitudes toward violence and death is often based on ideologies related, for example, to race (meaning we are less likely to value and thus grieve the loss of Black lives), gender (meaning we are less likely to value and thus grieve the lives of transgendered folks), and sex (meaning we are less likely to take seriously the particular forms of violence meted out against women).

This feeling of indifference maintains distance between us and numbs our consciences and weakens any sense of responsibility, let alone response, we take. To justify grieving the lost lives or violence against vulnerable groups requires a collective struggle, a collective reminder that their lives do not mean less but rather are indeed our concern and responsibility.

Made in the image of God, our humanity is reflected in our capacity for relation with others. Being distanced from one another alienates us from God and from the truest forms of ourselves. Spirit murder mars our moral imagination and the image of God that is reflected within each of us. A cultural ethos that allows spirit murder also allows us not to lament the violence and death we see sustained by the most vulnerable in society. Parents who are committed to the physical, spiritual, and moral well-being of their children must combat these tendencies.

One way to parent toward justice is to foster in our children a robust moral imagination that enables them to embrace the grievability of the most vulnerable by attempting to build intimacy in the everyday with them. We might consider, then, the social and political power of intimacy, and how it helps us to embrace an understanding of mourning as protest.[70]

---

[69]Judith Butler, *The Force of Non-Violence: An Ethico-Political Bind* (New York: Verso Books, 2020), 75.
[70]Ibid., 76.

Building Intimacy in the Everyday

A daily protest of lament undermines those social beliefs that enable and perpetuate our indifference to violence against life. Promoting *intimacy*—or sharing vulnerability—between our children and those deemed nobodies is key to developing such a moral imagination in our children. Though the term "intimacy" is associated with romantic relationships and sexuality, I invite us to think of intimacy more broadly. Intimacy, at its core, is sharing vulnerability. Intimacy in *all* our relationships enables us to regard ourselves as deeply interconnected with others, to realize that our own well-being is connected to and reliant upon the other. This type of intimacy allows us to be open to the possibility of being able to be "undone" by others. Rather than something negative, being "undone" by another "can take the form of grief and mourning, desire and ecstasy, solidarity and empathy, and mutual regard."[71] Encouraging intimacy can then be a way to build, restore, or maintain relationship with the other. It can be a pathway to resisting spirit murder, to becoming more fully human, more fully engaged in action that reflects the gospel.

In the gospels, we encounter a Christ who is concerned with the most poor and vulnerable in society, one who associates with and heals those considered untouchable, castaways, or sinners. Examples of Jesus healing those who are sick (such as the cleansing of a leper and the hemorrhaging woman) come to mind. The social context of Jesus' time often associated illness with sin. Perceiving illness and suffering as punishment for wrongdoing, people maintained distance and shunned untouchables. Jesus challenges this way of being by offering grace and healing to these folks, sometimes to the chagrin of those in power (e.g., religious authorities perturbed by Jesus' performing healing on the Sabbath). The gospels are clear that Jesus not only acted in these ways but also asks us, his followers, to do so.

While Jesus sometimes spoke plainly about concern for the poor, he more often used parables to teach and preach. As short stories with a moral lesson, his parables invited listeners to imagine a more just reality and assess their own role in hastening that reality. When his disciples asked him why he spoke in parables, Jesus said:

---

[71]Nash, *Black Feminism Reimagined,* 117.

"Seeing they do not perceive, and hearing they do not listen, nor do they understand." With them indeed is fulfilled the prophecy of Isaiah that says:

"You will indeed listen, but never understand, and you will indeed look, but never perceive.

For this people's heart has grown dull, and their ears are hard of hearing, and they have shut their eyes..."

But blessed are your eyes, for they see, and your ears, for they hear." (Matthew 13:13-16. My emphasis.)

Jesus used stories from everyday reality to teach people whose minds had become dulled or who turned their eyes from those who suffer. Jesus encourages us to resist and challenge the numbing pathologies that accompany "spirit murder" and to share in the beauty of intimacies being created and sustained with those most vulnerable.

That Jesus used parables to inspire our imaginations should not be surprising. Because we learn through storytelling and particularly through stories that reflect the everyday realities of own cultures, with my children I likewise use stories and examples from *lo cotidiano*, our "everyday" lives. It is a concept that *mujerista* (Latina feminists in the United States) theologian Ada María Isasi-Díaz developed.

As a theological concept, *lo cotidiano* suggests that we can shape our actions, see and know God by examining what is happening in our society in the everyday, especially if we are attentive to the everyday struggles of the most poor and vulnerable. A commitment to engaging with the everyday realities of the oppressed empowers us to do what many parents find difficult to do—acknowledge, engage, explain, and lament the violence they see around them. Such engagement helps us to understand not only the lived reality of the poor and vulnerable but also the ways that we relate to the structures of violence that make them poor and vulnerable in our society, the structures that tempt us to turn away, to disconnect, not to mourn. Thus, *lo cotidiano* refers to the daily oppressions sustained by marginalized groups. It allows us to be open to witnessing oppression and to begin to "imagine a different world, a different social structure, a different way of relating to the divine…a different way of relating to ourselves: who we are and what we do,"[72] as well as how we regard and relate to others.

In these ways, attention to *lo cotidiano* aids us in creating intimacy between ourselves, our children, and those whom our society deems to have no value. Such attention prompts us to engage the lives of the vulnerable as part of our own everyday and ordinary life. What does this look like in our everyday lives with our children?

Conversations of Mourning and Imagination

I regularly have conversations with all my children about justice as it relates to race/ethnicity, gender, and sexuality. As it relates to race, for example, my children understand the concerns and overarching goals of the Movement for Black Lives. Rather than hiding terrible news from them, I have age-appropriate conversations with them about it. For example, in the wake of protests collectively mourning the murder of George Floyd, a Black man from Minneapolis, I talked with my children. They know that Derek Chauvin, a white police officer, killed Floyd because he was suspected of using a fake twenty-dollar bill. They know that Chauvin murdered Floyd by keeping his knee on Floyd's neck for nine minutes and twenty-nine seconds. They understand that Chauvin utterly disregarded the value of Floyd's life. They know that such violence is not an exception, that others consistently dehumanize Black persons and other persons of color, and perceive them as criminals, menaces, animals. Such dehumanization makes it easier to place these persons into the category of those who are ungrievable. My children know that the protests of the Movement for Black Lives (MLB) are necessary collective expressions of grief for those deemed ungrievable. These protests offer an essential counter-message, one that describes Black lives intimately, and one that names the changes necessary to bring about a world in which Black lives really do matter. Messages like this shape mourning as protest and shape the conversations we have with our children. They resist spirit murder and forge intimacy with everyday practices of imagination.

---

[72]Ada María Isasi-Díaz, "Mujerista Discourse: A Platform for Latina's Subjugated Knowledge," in *Decolonizing Epistemologies: Latina/o Theology and Philosophy*, eds. Ada María Isasi-Díaz and Eduardo Mendieta (New York: Fordham University Press, 2012), 54–55.

After Floyd's murder, I began by telling my sons that a police officer had killed yet another Black man. My sons are very young, so I used terms and concepts they can understand. I explained, "George Floyd was a man who was a daddy, who used to drive trucks and work as a security guard. He was also a Black man who got very hurt today. So hurt that he died. A police officer hurt him, and it seems as if he did that for a very silly reason." This, of course, led to questions. My sons asked me why this had happened. Because theirs was largely a rhetorical question, I pressed them: "Well, what do *you* think?" My sons were able to identify that this was about Floyd's race.

As early as pre-school I had been explaining to them the ways that Black persons and other persons of color are sometimes treated very differently, that many people think that skin color can mean that someone is bad, and so forth. In doing so, I was able to point to *lo cotidiano* of the struggles of persons of color and help my children not only understand this but challenge it. So, in response to my "What do you think?" they suggested, "It was probably because he was a Black man." I affirmed this response but followed up with more questions: "Why would you say that?" Talking over one another they explained how sometimes Black people are not treated fairly and how some people think they are scary and how these feelings make some people not care about Black people as much. I affirmed this response and then, importantly, asked them how such treatment made them feel. They said that it made them feel sad for him and now he can't be a daddy anymore. This was crucial. My boys were identifying the human Floyd was, the relationships that he had, and were considering the impact this would leave. They were empathetic about George Floyd's family, and especially his children, never being able to be with him again. My youngest noted that he would be very sad if he could not hug *me* again. That Floyd *may* have used a counterfeit bill was not the point (folks often attempt to justify police killing Black persons by creating a dehumanizing narrative of criminality, which numbs us to the reality of their humanity). The point was that my sons knew that Floyd likely would have made it out of that encounter alive had he not been Black, that Floyd was a human—like them, like us—with hopes, fears, and relationships that were shattered under the pressure of Chauvin's knee. They connected with this shared humanity, and they mourned the human who was George Floyd; and in so doing they were able to tap more deeply into what it means to be made in God's image.

In our family when tragedy strikes or additional prayer or devotion is needed, we often light candles. We lit a candle for George Floyd that evening and every evening until the candle was gone. This was wonderful: Each day the boys argued over whose turn it was to light the candle! Importantly, our honoring Floyd did not end with lighting a candle. In our continuing conversations I asked my boys what they think needs to happen so that more people don't get hurt and killed. I asked what they think we could or should do. In other words, I was attempting to inculcate a sense that resistance ought to happen, but that we must first imagine how we can do this. We will not simply settle for the status quo, allowing violence to go unchecked. We will push ourselves out of rage and grief to consider and/or demand a different reality. The possibilities named by my sons were: We could teach people that Black people are not bad and teach police to not hurt or hit (this is a general principle in our home). I followed up by encouraging them to imagine how things could have gone differently. I would say things like, "Okay, boys, tell me how that could have ended without George getting hurt." or "What do you think the rules should be when a police officer stops a person?" In this way, I aim to help them imagine making changes in society, politics, and in policy. This is protest.

I have had similar conversations with my daughter, who is much older and understands a more sophisticated analysis of our current pathological social ideologies. For example, she can understand the concept of "intersectionality," a term created by Kimberlé Crenshaw that notes that the benefits that occur with privileged identities and the difficulties that occur with marginalized identities often overlap and reinforce one another. So, while white women suffer from continued gender oppression, they still bear the privilege of whiteness whereas a woman of color bears the overlapping oppressions of gender and race. These intersections are important to enumerate if we do not want to reduce individual experiences. My daughter is aware of this and can speak intelligently about the overlapping and reinforcing oppressions that occur at the intersections of race, ethnicity, gender, sexuality, class, and nationality.

This concept recently enabled my daughter to make a wonderful presentation in one of her high school classes about the hashtag #sayhername. The #sayhername campaign was driven by the lack of visibility of Black women who are also killed by police at disproportionate rates. The intersections of their race, gender, and, at times, class make them less likely to be discussed, less likely to be mourned. Because I am raising my children in an environment where having such discussions are the norm, as they grow they'll be more likely to question and call out injustice when and where they see it.

A brief example: My daughter is a gamer and is often online with other teenagers who sometimes use racist, sexist, nationalist discourse against others on the site. I have listened proudly to her clearly and convincingly tell her peers, "What you just said was racist and sexist. You should apologize to him/her/them." She has been removed from online play groups for this reason, but she has remained firm in her resolve not to allow such behavior to go unchecked. In this sense, encouraging the imagining of a different world also inspires our children to inspire this in others. Experiencing the 2017 Women's March with her was beautiful, but it was neither the beginning nor the end of lessons in fighting for social justice.

With my daughter and with her younger siblings, I encourage protest via the very vulnerable human act of intimacy. A just moral imagination is not constructed with a "one and done" protest. It is formed by consistent witness to the ugliest of events oppressed persons bear in *lo cotidiano,* by strategic and compassionate framing and questioning that enables rather than stifles their ability to remain intimately connected to their fellow humans and to mourn.

Try It Out

I have provided a few examples of the ways that my children and I approach creating intimacy with oppressed persons and how that is important for shaping a just and robust moral imagination. Following are the steps that I typically take; you may wish to complete them in a different order, or remove some steps altogether. All families are different, and you will know what your child can handle and how best to approach them.

1. **Bear Witness:** Because bearing witness is easier said than done, many parents do not speak to their children about racism, sexism, and so on. The first step in this practice is therefore to engage and discuss consistently the *cotidiano* or daily reality of the most

vulnerable. There may be a specific event you would like to discuss with your child (e.g., the murder of George Floyd, particular flooding and wildfires exacerbated by climate change), or you may want to have a more general conversation about a particular injustice. The point here is to refuse to shy away from difficult conversations. Use age-appropriate words to bear witness with your child.

2. **Engage Emotion, or Promote Intimacy:** The violence and injustice we see around us are aided by the dehumanization of the marginalized and the justification of disconnection, or lack of intimacy. So, we have to engage our children's emotions so that they remain open to and regard the humanity of the other. You can begin by explaining how the injustice makes you feel. Yes, we must be vulnerable before our children, too. This practice will likely broaden their sense of intimacy with the most vulnerable as well as strengthen the intimacy between you and your child. Ask them how they feel, too. Be sure that you have included stories about the real humans behind the injustices (e.g., George Floyd was a dad who had a history, who had a particular job and family, who was made in the image of God, who also happened to be Black). Providing such stories about people will enable your children to remain connected and focused upon their shared humanity.

3. **Encourage Imagination and Action:** The final step is to ask your children questions that require them to imagine a different way that the world can be. These questions can be local or global. All that matters here is that the questions encourage them to imagine. Questions such as "What do you think we should/could do?" "How do you think we could change this situation?" and "How could this have been different?" are excellent conversation starters. Actions that can be taken may come from these conversations. Encourage your children to engage in action and, when possible, do it with them. This might mean performing charitable acts, or marching in the streets, or holding a workshop at church, or writing to your congressperson, or voting. Action is important. Helping children see that it isn't all hopeless, that there are many people trying to do good and change the violence around us, is crucial.

11

Meditation with Collage

Ellen Ott Marshall and Katherine Marshall

Justice work is emotional work, a roller coaster of excitement, frustration, determination, discouragement, anger, and grief. For relatively privileged people, like the two of us, it often involves feelings of guilt, complicity, embarrassment, and even shame as well. All of these emotions are important, and it's crucial to pay attention to them. However, if we participate in activism focused more on our own emotions than on the lives of people experiencing injustice, then our emotions become unhelpful, even distracting and obstructive. To address this challenge, we—a white mother and daughter in the US—describe a practice of meditation using collage. Like all forms of engaged meditation, this practice helps participants engage the world rather than withdraw from it. Meditation with collage can help all people process all kinds of experiences, but here we suggest it as a practice particularly for white and otherwise privileged families to process emotions at home so that we do not center them in public.

Outrage and Complicity

In October 2016, our family sat on the couch watching a recording of then-candidate Donald Trump bragging about grabbing women by the "pussy." I (Ellen) felt the assault of his words full force on my chest just as twelve-year-old Katherine said, "He's a monster." When Trump was elected, we were furious and incredibly sad. We celebrated Katherine's thirteenth birthday at the Women's March in Atlanta on January 21, 2017. Both sets of grandparents attended with us, supporting Katherine's growing political awareness and determination to resist injustice. The march gave all of us a means to express our outrage that this person who so blatantly transgressed our values, sense of decency, and Christian commitments now occupied the White House. It also placed us in the company of people determined to resist everything that his administration represented and pledged to do. In the coming months and years, we wrote letters, signed petitions, and joined actions for racial justice, immigrant rights, reproductive freedom, and voter engagement.

As Katherine grew from a twelve-year-old girl to a young woman of seventeen, a growing understanding of the problematic role that white women like us often play in social movements complicated her feelings of outrage and determination. Voter data crystallized this for us: White Christian women continued to support Trump no matter what he said or did. It was easy, of course, to distinguish ourselves from "those other white women," but we had to acknowledge that relatively privileged people like us have the power to passively benefit from the status quo whenever it serves us. In a very real and problematic way, participating in social justice activism is optional for us. As relatively affluent, straight, white, cisgender[73] women, we occupy a social location that benefits from several forms of systemic injustice. We can actively resist injustice, or we can exercise the privilege of our race/ethnic identity, class, and traditional family structure and remain complicit. We found that the more we understood about our social location in relationship to our commitments to justice, the more emotionally complicated things became. We knew that we needed to attend to these emotions, understand the realities that give rise to them, and figure out how to work constructively with them. But how?

Along with many of the other developments that took place during my teenage years, I (Katherine) joined most of my peers on various social media platforms. It is impossible to exclude social media from a conversation about activism because platforms such as Instagram and Facebook are central to many social justice movements. Social media

---

[73]Cisgender means that one's gender identity aligns with one's biological, sexual anatomy at birth.

allows for a mass dispersal of information, so social justice movements can grow rapidly on the platforms. However, I have also found online activism to be extremely frustrating and full of contradictions.

During the summer of 2020, my feed was full of resources and news about Black Lives Matter, and it was inspiring to see my online community, which is almost entirely kids of my generation, be so impassioned about the rise of anti-racist protests following the police murders of George Floyd, Ahmaud Arbury, Breonna Taylor, and others.

Then, I started to notice some patterns that made me feel less excited. I saw people post accusatory messages, targeting those who were posting various resources, calling out users for "performative activism." However, those same people also expressed frustration and judgment toward users who weren't posting anything at all. People were criticized for not posting *and* for posting the wrong things. In the midst of this contradiction, it felt like everyone was yelling at one another in a very unproductive way. It made me want to withdraw from social media altogether. I realized that the anticipation of other people's negative reactions governed my decisions about whether to participate and what to say. I had to learn to trust myself with posting or not posting certain messages or resources. And I had to risk making mistakes, learning from them, and trying again.[74]

These interactions on social media confirmed the need to do some serious emotional work, and to do this work at home and offline to avoid the mistake of centering *our* feelings in public. When white people respond to accusations of racism by talking about how the criticism makes us feel, we impede the work of justice by centering ourselves. When privileged people focus attention on our feelings of guilt or defensiveness, we impede the work of justice by centering ourselves. As Ruby Hamad explains in her book, *White Tears, Brown Scars,* we white women in particular impede social justice by weaponizing our emotions.[75] When we are challenged on our racism, for example, we draw attention to our feelings of embarrassment, sadness, guilt, anger, and self-righteousness rather than listening

---

[74]For a wonderful resource on working with youth for peace and justice, see Elizabeth W. Corrie, *Youth Ministry as Peace Education: Overcoming Silence, Transforming Violence* (Minneapolis, MN: Fortress Press, 2021).

[75]Ruby Hamad, *White Tears/Brown Scars: How White Feminism Betrays Women of Color* (New York: Catapult, 2020).

openly to the experiences and criticism being shared with us. We lean into the role of the vulnerable white woman by claiming to be a victim or under threat, and garner sympathy for our distress. And we do all of this at the expense of the people actually experiencing the systemic injustice that benefits us. In these various ways—whether subconsciously or strategically disruptive—white women like us siphon energy from the movement and attention from those whose experiences should guide us.

To state the obvious, this chapter risks repeating the error. So, we want to be clear: White and otherwise privileged people have emotional work to do *and* we need to do this work at home so that we can pay deep attention to the feelings and experiences of other people in public. This chapter describes a practice for doing precisely this.

Emotions, Faith, and Activism

Emotional development is not easy for parents or for kids, but it is familiar work for all of us. What may be new—or require more intentional practice—is integrating this emotional work with faith and framing it all as part of activism. We find this kind of integration and framing to be deeply true and also both helpful and challenging. Faith and activism are connected in our baptismal covenant, which calls us to "strive for justice and peace among all people and respect the dignity of every human being."[76] We take this commitment to be as central to baptism as the water itself. We have also been formed in a tradition that teaches that the work of striving for justice includes practices of confession for "what we have done and what we have left undone."[77] And we experience weekly communion as a moment of grace and rededication to all of the works of justice and faith. Even in our church, which is a typically reserved Episcopalian one, we experience a range of emotions in the liturgy itself. And, most importantly, we absorb into our bodies the teaching that striving for justice, confessing shortcomings, receiving grace, and trying again make up the rhythm of faith and life.

---

[76]"Holy Baptism," *The Book of Common Prayer and Administration of the Sacraments and Other Rites and Ceremonies of the Church* (New York: Church Publishing, 1979), 305.

[77]"Daily Morning Prayer Rite 2," *The Book of Common Prayer and Administration of the Sacraments and Other Rites and Ceremonies of the Church* (New York: Church Publishing, 1979), 79.

Although we do not spend a lot of time with the Bible in our house, there is one story in particular that speaks to the feelings and the work we are trying to describe in this chapter. It's the story of the persistent widow and the unrighteous judge recorded in the gospel according to Luke. Listen again to how Jesus tells his disciples this story at a time when they were feeling discouraged:

> He said, "In a certain city there was a judge who neither feared God nor had any respect for people. In that city there was a widow who kept coming to him and saying, 'Grant me justice against my opponent.' For a while he refused; but later he said to himself, 'Though I have no fear of God and no respect for anyone, yet because this widow keeps bothering me, I will grant her justice, so that she may not wear me out by continually coming.'" And the Lord said, "Listen to what the unjust judge says. And will not God grant justice to God's chosen ones who cry to God day and night? Will God delay long in helping them? I tell you, God will quickly grant justice to them. And yet, when the Son of Man comes, will he find faith on earth?" (Luke 18:2–8)

I (Ellen) have always loved this parable. I feel inspired by the persistence and courage of the widow, and I love that Jesus presents her as a model of faithfulness. Through this story, Jesus praises relentless advocacy for justice and connects it with faithfulness in a way that is powerful and encouraging. Faithfulness looks like relentless persistence in the pursuit of justice; it looks like continually bothering those with power until they do the right thing.

But there is, of course, something else going on in this parable, something that also rings true in a more sobering way. I want to stand with the widow, to march alongside her, to join her relentless pursuit of justice. But I need to acknowledge that the widow is also marching toward me, challenging me, "bothering" me. As a straight, relatively affluent, white woman in the US, I need to acknowledge that I have forms of power that put me on the receiving end of advocacy. In Hamad's words, "White women can oscillate between their gender and their race, between being the oppressed and being the oppressor."[78] And as a parent, I need to equip my white kids both to follow the lead

---

[78]Hamad, *White Tears/Brown Scars,* 14.

of the widow and also to respond with openness when she challenges us.[79] Among other things, this means that we all need to develop a capacity to work constructively with the reality that different things can be true at the same time. For example, I can both contribute to justice work and impede it at the same time. I can be outraged at unfair systems and be embarrassed by how I benefit from them at the same time. I can feel inspired to make a difference and contrite about a mistake at the same time.

Acknowledging these contradictions does not affirm them as good or cement them as unchangeable. But it does, importantly, recognize that different facets of our identity situate us in multiple ways in the context of social movements and social change. This means that we need to expect to feel challenged even as we challenge others, to be criticized even when we are being critical, to experience guilt even when we denounce wrong-doing. We need to prepare for the widow turning to face us. We need to learn from the emotions that her challenge raises in us without displacing her challenge with our emotions. Feelings are natural features of human experience, valuable sources of knowledge, good and healthy dimensions of life. We are not discouraging or disparaging emotions. But we are underscoring the necessity of reflecting on them in private so that we do not center them in public.

Meditation and Collage

In our separate rooms most mornings Katherine and I practice engaged meditation, which has a long history in Buddhism and in Christianity.[80] We practice meditation in order to participate fully and constructively in the world, not to escape from it. Meditation practices help us to see the connections between our interior lives and our actions, and we know that careful attention to the interior life helps us to be more grounded, responsive, courageous, and open as we participate in the world. We perceive—and try to live out—a

---

[79]Another incredibly helpful resource for parents of white kids is Jennifer Harvey, *Raising White Kids: Bringing Up Children in a Racially Unjust America* (Nashville, TN: Abingdon Press, 2017).

[80]See Thich Nhat Hanh, *Peace Is Every Step: The Path of Mindfulness in Everyday Life* (New York: Bantam Books, 1991); Thich Nhat Hanh, *Being Peace*, 2nd ed. (Berkeley, CA: Parallax Press, 2005); and Andrew Dreitcer, *Living Compassion: Loving Like Jesus* (Nashville: Upper Room Books, 2017).

constant movement between meditation and action, between faith and advocacy. Meditation helps us to pause to reflect, to re-center, and to remember our place in the scheme of things. It helps us to work constructively with the emotional parts of ourselves and the emotional dimensions of activism.

We meditate in different ways. I (Ellen) sometimes follow a particular practice such as centering prayer, which has a structure that includes readings, reflection on a sacred word, and intentional practices of stilling the mind. Sometimes I sit in silence with a small stone that fits perfectly in my fingers and simply breathe. Sometimes I read poetry and let my mind linger over the words and the feelings they generate. Sometimes I have particular concerns that I journal and pray about. For me (Katherine), movement is really helpful as a practice of meditation. I've found that syncing breath and movement in a yoga practice is extremely centering, especially first thing in the morning when the house is quiet. After moving, I sit and breathe or scan my body for areas of tension. Other times, I listen to guided scanning or breathing meditations. Journaling before I go to bed is another form of meditation because it gives me the opportunity to empty my mind of worries and fixations and to become fully present to the world once more.

You and your family should try out different kinds of things and land on whatever seems to help you create and hold a space for reflection, for centering, for stillness. In the remaining pages of this chapter, we offer another resource that you can integrate into your meditation to process contradictory experiences and emotions in particular.[81] Collage is an art form that is likely familiar to most families. In our house, all three of our kids have, at some point, torn up pictures or tissue paper and glued them onto a piece of paper. For a history project once, Katherine's teacher asked students to create a collage

---

[81]For art as a resource for theological practice with Black youth see: Anne E. Streaty Wimberly and Sarah Farmer, *Raising Hope: Four Paths to Courageous Living for Black Youth* (Nashville: United Methodist Board of General Higher Education, 2017). Another scholar in religious education who works with collage and contradictions explicitly is Lauren Calvin Cooke. For her dissertation research, Cooke explored the book of Job with youth by inviting them to make theological collages as a way to process contradictions. Lauren Calvin Cooke, "Wisdom's Pedagogy: Engaging Biblical Wisdom Literature with Young People" (unpublished manuscript, last modified February 14, 2022), Microsoft Word file.

that would capture the paradoxical nature of US identity. Katherine centered her collage on the paradox of freedom. As we talked about her project, it struck us that collage might be a helpful tool that we could integrate into our meditation practice at times when we need to process contradictions. Collage is a medium that allows for contradictions: You can incorporate different kinds of images onto one page without needing to resolve them. These contradictory things or paradoxical ideas can occupy one space, which creates a challenging and important resource for reflection.

Many meditation practices rely on an object of focus, something that you bring to your awareness and practice holding in the center. We suggest that collage can serve as an object of focus for this emotional work, especially when the emotions one needs to process are somehow contradictory or paradoxical—such as outrage and complicity. Collage is an art form that can express and hold contradiction. As a meditative exercise, it can be a practice that helps you express and explore the different feelings you and your children have. As a centering object for a meditation practice, the completed collage can focus your thoughts and help you to linger over images to see what new feelings and ideas arise from them.

For some of you, the process of making a collage might be a meditative experience. Like Katherine, you might find that assembling the materials provides you the space and structure that you need to reflect, to find stillness, and to feel grounded. Others of you, like Ellen, might find that the completed collage serves as a centering object for meditation. When I (Ellen) meditate with a centering object like this, I get comfortable in my chair and use a little lap desk to hold the thing on which I am trying to focus. That lets me rest my gaze comfortably. I give myself some time to center, taking time to breathe and move toward stillness. Meditating on or with art is an unpredictable and open-ended experience, and it is important to let the feelings and thoughts arise as they will. The point is to create and hold a space where you can reflect honestly with yourself about hard feelings and hard truths so that you can enter the public spaces ready to center other people and respond to them and their concerns with *openness* and *courage*. Our hope for all of us who both stand with the widow and receive her challenge is that we can respond to her challenge with courage, centering her, centering the work she needs us to do, and faithfully, persistently doing it.

Creating a Space

Throughout our description of this process, we have frequently used the phrase "creating a space." That is intentional and important language for us. We need both space and structure in our lives to process experiences so that we can respond well. Our culture moves very quickly, demands immediate responses, and is generally impatient with reflection and unforgiving of mistakes. While we find meditation to be intrinsically helpful and healthy, we also understand it to be a form of resistance to a culture that is so intent on reducing complexity, issuing snap judgments, and perpetuating frenetic patterns of engagement. Our world also has urgent problems demanding response, and we know that those with power and privilege use all manner of methods to resist and delay change. It is crucial that we do the interior work that helps us to be better agents of change rather than using the interior work as an excuse, escape, or impediment. This means that we can't remain in a reflective mode. Rather, we understand reflection and action to be two parts of the same work and try to integrate them in our lives. We need to be very clear with ourselves and our communities that we practice daily meditation not for its own sake or for our own peace of mind, but in order to bring our best selves to the urgent and vital work for justice. When we take time to process emotions, we are better able to receive challenges without defensiveness, to listen openly to feedback, and to respond with a genuine willingness to change ourselves and structures.

Like so many dimensions of faith and activism, this work is ongoing and requires practice. That is why it is practical for families. Engaging justice by processing emotions at home builds on familiar family homework: We talk about the day, we think through challenges, we share mistakes, we generate ideas, we prepare to try new things and risk hard things, we comfort and reassure and challenge one another, we articulate and enact values, and we gear up to enter the world with commitments to make it better. In other words, we ride the roller coaster of parenting and activism together. But we also pause the ride, check one another, process the ups and downs, revisit purpose and process, and remember how to get out of the way and bring our best selves to the work of change.

So, we invite you to think about how your family might create spaces to process the emotions that accompany the work of justice. Maybe tear up some pieces of paper together and see what clarity you find through messy and mindful collage.

Try It Out

When I (Katherine) sit down to create a collage, I always begin with a goal in mind, an intention for the piece. In some cases, the intention is as simple as creating a visually appealing piece of art. At other times, it is more complicated, like creating a feeling that I want to carry into a new month or year. For the purpose of processing contradictory emotions around activism, the intention may be to express the contradictions you feel. There is not a wrong way to do this. I've found that I have completed a collage when I feel as if my emotions have been adequately represented on the page. Continue tweaking the collage until you feel as if your thoughts and emotions have been emptied onto the page, giving you a sense of relief. These are the steps I follow.

1. **Collect Materials**

    a. You can use a combination of pictures from magazines and catalogues, markers, colored paper, patterned paper, fabric, stickers, etc.

    b. I like using many different materials to make the collage more interesting. For a meditation practice, it may also be effective to use more materials to illustrate a sense of tension.

2. **Start with a Word**

    a. What is one word or phrase that has been popping up in your head in the midst of your contradictory emotions? For my project about American identity, I chose "freedom."

    b. You can write this word in the middle of your collage or just keep it to the side, remembering that it is the guiding word for your project.

3. **Play Around**

    a. Try positioning your materials in different places on the page. Try different things, and continue moving the pieces around, adding them and taking them away until you've adequately captured what your word means to you in this moment.

b. This is where the real meditation and processing of emotions takes place. Don't watch TV while you're doing this. Think about what you feel and *why* you feel that way. How can you capture that in images and words? It may be helpful to journal for a few minutes before setting your pieces into place in order to get a better idea of how your emotions look as words.

4. **Secure Pieces**

a. Glue everything in place.

5. **Finish**

a. Now, you may want to pray or meditate over your final project.

b. How do you feel now compared to when you began?

c. Journal about your experience or explain it to a family member. It may be easier to talk about these emotions now that you have illustrated them.

d. Refrain from posting pictures of your artwork on social media or sharing it with a bunch of people. The purpose of this project is to process emotions at home. Keep it here. It stays sacred that way.

12

Community Organising

Keith Hebden with Martha Hebden

Over the course of many years, I (Keith) was involved in various forms of political protest from marches, blockades, and occupations to disrupting far-right events. It was exciting, felt meaningful, and was spiritually nourishing. But I became increasingly uneasy about two things: First, nearly everyone in the protest movement looked and sounded like me. We were mostly white, middle-class, educated protesters up against blue-collar police—without a decision maker in the crowd. Second, we never won the argument or achieved structural change. So I began to ask myself: Is this worth it? Is this how I should be investing my time? I had also begun to read New Testament scholar Walter Wink, who argued that Jesus took a third way between violence and passivity—nonviolent resistance. He in turn pointed me to Gene Sharp's more pragmatic nonviolence. Sharp became disillusioned with moral pacifism and developed a research base looking at how nonviolence can be a practical way to resist injustice.[82] Wink also discussed Saul Alinsky's *Reveille for Radicals,* which I then read and found nothing short of life-changing. Alinsky pioneered what we now call broad-based community organising, which involves building the power of civil society institutions such as churches, community groups, and schools to win incremental change in local neighbourhoods. Alinsky argued for diversity, accountability, pragmatism, and never doing for others what they can do for themselves.

---

[82]For more information, see Walter Wink, *Jesus and the Third Way* (Minneapolis, MN: Fortress Press, 2003); Gene Sharp, *The Politics of Nonviolent Action* (Boston: Sargent Publisher, 1973); Saul Alinsky, *Rules for Radicals: A Practical Primer for Realistic Radicals* (New York: Random House, 1971); and Saul Alinsky, *Reveille for Radicals* (New York: Vintage Books, 1989).

As a result, I found myself shifting from mobilised protest to engagement in broad-based community organising—a shift that coincided with my children getting to an age at which the risk of my going to prison became a serious consideration. I started organising with people to build relational power to bring about change; and the more I organised, the more change I saw, without spending so much as a single night in a police cell. More importantly, my children started to become involved in politics alongside adults as equals. While Bethany and Martha have both taught me much about faith and public life, Martha has so far been the most engaged in politics. This chapter is built around one of our conversations in which, at fourteen and forty-five respectively, we reflect on what we've learned together about politics, building power, and bringing about social change. We are sharing this with you to encourage you to get involved as parents and as families in Community Organising—whatever that might look like in your local context and community.

The Limitations of Protest

Without a robust theory of change, protest rarely achieves the results it sets out to. There is a place for movement-based political activism, and when patient grassroots organising comes together with the spontaneous uprising approach, it can be effective.[83] But we do not want to train another generation that social activism is more about moral victory—being seen to be doing the "right thing"—than about making substantive change. Marching, blockades, and public liturgical protest—such as when I took a group of thirty ordinands to a lamentation at the nuclear weapons factory in Berkshire, UK—can agitate the protester to change, but it can also, conversely, condition them for a lifetime of impotently kicking against power if protest without winning change becomes a habit. We can do more harm than good by teaching them that protest is about demonstrating against unchangeable injustice, as this part of our conversation reveals:

Keith: What's your earliest memory of politics and of public faith?

Martha: The [anti-]Drones protest with Ruth and Ellie…Mum explained before the protest what we were going to and why. And I thought

[83]See Mark Engler and Paul Engler, *This Is an Uprising: How Nonviolent Revolt Is Shaping the Twenty-first Century* (New York: Bold Type Books, 2016).

it was very important to protest about, and then Ellie and Ruth were very passionate about the protest, and we made banners.

Keith: In Lincoln.

Martha: Yeh. And Ellie was shouting. And there were loads of banners and posters and people shouting and being angry.

Keith: And why is it you particularly remember Ellie shouting?

Martha: She was very loud, and people were responding to her.

Keith: Yeah, she invented a chant that everyone joined in with and it ended up on banners and stuff.

Martha: Yeah. And I was feeling like we were a community and ... I was a part of something because we were all doing the same thing for the same reason. And I do remember thinking, *I know that I'm sad and angry about what's happening, but I don't know how this is helping.*

Keith: Huh, that's an interesting question I think most adults don't ask. I was going through that same questioning process over several years. Which is why I got involved in organising—because I kept thinking, 'I don't know how this is helping.' Because no decision-makers were present.

After this protest against drone warfare, I took part in direct action against the military base at the same location. Along with five others, we used wire cutters to make a gateway of peace into the site and to set up a vigil for Afghani children killed by allied drones. The biggest impact on my children was the subsequent police raid on our home while I was in custody. The raid was disproportionate. Church members saw five officers turn up at the vicarage—our home—and remove bags, boxes, notebooks, and posters. The children were fine: When I arrived home the next evening, then seven-year-old Martha, who had lectured the officers on why military drones shouldn't have been deployed, greeted me with, "Daddy the police have been. Come and see: Your office is so tidy!" Our direct action did have an effect in this case: The heavy-handedness of the police, both on that day and in court, helpfully demonstrated to a wider audience the general problem of peace by domination. Their attitude led to public and private conversations around drone warfare and disproportionate state violence that would have been difficult to initiate otherwise. But the consequences could have been serious.

Community Organising as Effective Nonviolent Resistance

If protest alone is an unreliable and risky mechanism for bringing about change, what practice might we engage in as parents and families instead of—or perhaps in addition to—protest? I discovered a clue hidden away in Matthew's gospel in the short phrase of Jesus: "But I say to you, Do not resist an evildoer" (Matthew 5:38). Walter Wink surprisingly translates this as "Do not resist evil by force"—and makes a case that Jesus was not suggesting we let evil run rampant, but rather that we resist evil through nonviolent means.[84] Some argue that Jesus was a pacifist, but I think the various gospel depictions of Jesus paint him as a pragmatist. He suggests that when we are faced with occupying forces (such as the Roman Empire) who have a virtual monopoly on violence, we need to be creative and agile in our response. Most of all we need to build solidarity: Train the crowds, heal the sick, mobilise an empowered people.

This is what I think Community Organising is all about—resisting evil through nonviolent means. In *How to Resist: Turn Protest to Power,* Matthew Bolton explores how Community Organising is a method of engagement undertaken by Citizens UK with around five hundred civic institutions across England and Wales.[85] They develop leaders of civic institutions to build a relational culture within and beyond their own organisation so they can listen deeply and develop leadership from within their community and negotiate directly with powerful decision makers. The basic building block of Community Organising is the relational meeting: a one-to-one conversation in which each person shares something of their public story to illustrate what drives them to act to discover common interest. It is also a space for mutual agitation and accountability so that politics is always rooted in personal relationship rather than just public policy or abstract opinion.

---

[84]Walter Wink, *Jesus and Nonviolence: A Third Way* (Minneapolis, MN: Fortress Press, 2003), 78.

[85]Matthew Bolton, *How to Resist: Turn Protest to Power* (London: Bloomsbury, 2017).

An Exciting, Participative Space for Children

One of the great things about Community Organising is the way children—even the very young—can participate in it fully. They can talk about their experience of injustice; they can explore solutions and build relational power; and they are deft at negotiating with decision makers. Adults can be reluctant to engage children in politics because we worry that they will be bored or confused, but it helpfully forces adults to simplify the complex issues in a way that is good for everyone. What's more, while children may not understand everything that is going on, they still appreciate being able to participate. They can look out at a roomful of people engaged in public life and feel exactly what all the adults are feeling, and it is just as exciting for them. From the age of seven, Martha absolutely loved being taken seriously by adults, without translation or mediation. My desire for all children to experience this drives much of my current organising work.

Keith: What's your earliest memory of Community Organising?

Martha: Doing the speech at the Maun Valley Citizens Assembly at the College. I remember I'd been getting the speech right in all the rehearsals and then on the day of the event I messed up.

Keith: Did you?!

Martha: Well, it was only a little bit, but I still remember it.

Keith: I think it was the bit about pension funds, which was really complicated, and you were seven.

Martha: Yeah, we had big buckets and we were taking money out of one bucket and putting it in another, talking about wages. And how it was unfair.

Keith: With Ralph.

Martha: Yeah. He was older than me and he was very good at talking. He was much better than me.

Keith: He was nine and you were seven.

Martha: Oh! I remember that before the assembly we were in your office, and a man came to your office and he was saying he wouldn't come to the assembly, and I asked him to come.

Keith: Yes! He said no to everyone else, but you had a prepared speech about road safety and your own personal journey to school, and then you said to him, "Will you come?" and he got all uncomfortable and then he folded. And he came. And then you spoke in front of 350 people at the assembly, and for a year every time we drove past it you got excited and said, "That's the place where I spoke to all those people."

Martha: I also remember the protest against housing charity, and we all wore big white suits.

Keith: That was interesting. There were sixty of us, and you were all wearing hazmat suits because we were saying Haven Homes was toxic and needed to clean up their act.

Martha: Yeah.

Keith: And there were only four children: you, your sister, and the two children and their mum who lived with us at the time.

Martha: Everyone was kind of panicky. And I remember I was with Mum and she was a bit panicky.

Keith: Yeah. Because there were vulnerably housed people who had been told by their landlord that we were trying to make them homeless. As we arrived, they were shouting and swearing and waving placards; they told us later they had been bussed in by the landlord and given cider and fee-waivers to take part. I managed to get both sides quiet long enough to talk about the difference between "Pax Romana," the fake type of peace-through-force that Haven Homes used to frighten people into not speaking out, and "Pax Christi," which is peace founded on justice and repaired relationships. Then I said, "Peace be with you!" and dozens replied, "And also with you"; and they respectfully shared the peace, shaking hands, hugging, healing the temporary divide, and uniting against the landlord.

Martha: Yeah, I remember that when we did the hugging and sharing the peace it went from being shouty to being peaceful.

Keith: And did you make the connection between that and what we do in church?

Martha: Yes, but I didn't think it was strange or normal, because I was young so whatever you do is just what you do; you don't have much of a sense of what is "normal" when you're young, you don't know what's going to happen, and you don't know if it's what normally happens. You just go along with it.

We changed both the meaning of "sharing the peace" and the power relationship in the protest. And we won! The housing provider was forced to fix up the flats/apartments; the mayor put an enquiry in place; and they built on that for further meaningful wins.

If you wanted to explain the difference between "Pax Romana" and "Pax Christi" to a child out of context, you would have a major challenge on your hands. But give children (and for that matter adults) a real substantive context in which to do their public faith, and we all grasp profound theological truths about what peace means in the Christian tradition and the way it is bound up with justice and restoring relationships rather than domination and the silencing of dissent. As a family, we live in a house where there is plenty of dissent, but it rarely disturbs the peace. But when I try to silence them—in one of my many clever ways—they recognise it for what it is—"Pax Romana"!

Workplace Organising—at School!

Martha was always keen to use what she learned about politics from the adults in her life and to translate it into her own world—to test it out in school. In Community Organising, the one-to-one relational conversation is the most radical thing we teach. Through such conversations, Martha started plotting her own political experiments.

Keith: You used a power analysis and "workplace organising" to become prime minister of your school.

Martha: Yes, in Year 5, in my primary/elementary school. We got loads of stickers and we gave them to people, and so they voted for me. I found children in every year group who other children respected and got them to vote for me and to give out stickers. And the lunch ladies got cross with me for handing out stickers.

Keith: Hah! You found all the relational leaders in each year group, and you got them on your side. Whereas I think all the other candidates just relied on their friends. And you won by a landslide. And you were really excited to have won.

Martha: And I hated being prime minister.

Keith: Why?

Martha: Because they didn't give me any actual power.

Keith: So, what did you learn from that?

Martha: That you don't get any power in schools unless you're an adult.

Keith: Maybe you can, but it takes a lot longer to build and you're not there for long.

Martha: And that I didn't care about getting power in primary school because I wasn't angry enough about any injustice.

Keith: You had a strong manifesto, but it was all stuff that if it didn't happen that was okay too.

Martha: I improved lunches. And I did say that people who were helping out in school, such as those looking after the younger year group, should have time for a proper lunch by getting a lunch reserved for them. And children who had been kind to others got a ticket that let them jump the lunch queue.

Keith: Yes! And you won that. Of all your policies, that one was properly put into action as a result of you being prime minister.

After she became prime minister, Martha discovered that it was not enough simply to have the title. Weekly, and then even daily, she spoke to the head teacher about the pledges and reminded her of their shared commitment to carry them out. Like Jesus' parable in Luke of the persistent widow and the unjust judge (Luke 18:1 –8), she could resist the head teacher's perceived slowness to act until she won real substantive change. What she had seen adults do in Community Organising, she put into practice in her (school) workplace.

Learning to Embrace "Cold" Anger

Martha has experienced both the exciting and the mundane aspects of Community Organising. To be resilient, it's good to know as soon as possible the hard reality of it. We've stood out in a car park in the rain directing delegates to a meeting, stacked chairs, and faced down angry white men—liberal activists and right-wing extremists. We've won and lost together. But what I really love is the ability to make talk about anger normal. Children, especially girls, are often taught that anger is negative. I want them to own anger with pride but not become disillusioned, bitter, and burnt out by it. In Community Organising settings, Martha gets to feel okay—good even—about her anger. She's seen, first-hand, the difference between "hot" or out-of-control anger, which is destructive, and "cold" anger—stoked anger that fires the furnace of action, providing motivation, energy, and passion to work for justice. I often teach the difference between these types of anger using the illustration of the burning bush that Moses encountered (Exodus 3). The burning bush represents the presence of God speaking to Moses about the injustice against God's people. The bush burns with this injustice. Yet as Moses comes closer, he notices, "the bush was blazing, yet it was not consumed" (Exodus 3:2). I want to encourage my children to allow anger that we continue to let burn without letting it consume us.

Keith: What's the biggest thing you've learned from organising?

Martha: That you need to have strong relationships with people. And that you need to have strong relationships with the right people. And you need to get them passionate about the change that you want to push or find people who are passionate about the thing you want to change. And then you find people in positions of power who have the authority to make the change. And then put lots of pressure on them alongside the people [with whom] you built power to make the change. Or find someone in power who is also wanting the change.

Keith: Have you seen that process done?

Martha: We went to a big church in Leicester. And there was a man outside who was angry because they thought it was...what was the word?

Keith: A hustings.

Martha: A hustings. But it wasn't. But they were protesting.

Keith: He was a party activist for a party whose candidate wasn't invited. He was shouting at me as one of the staff organisers, and you were with me. He was rude to everyone and he was angry. But it wasn't cold anger, it was hot anger, and he was just lashing out at everyone powerlessly.

Martha: When you're angry, you should use it constructively.

Keith: We were negotiating with mayoral candidates. Over the eighteen months before that, though, you helped make that meeting with mayoral candidates possible by helping me organise the alliance and coming to Leicester Citizens meetings.

Witnessing that Testimony against the Powerful Can Turn Enemies into Allies

Another valuable lesson we have all learned as a family is that testimony against the powerful can turn enemies into allies—a very useful tool in building power to bring about social change. Martha and Bethany have been part of several "Accountability Assemblies," which involve testimony from people experiencing injustice. The people who offer testimony have often helped lead or build the team, generated the solutions, and built the power ahead of the event. The testimony exposes decision makers publicly to the difference their actions or inactions make on real people, and the person giving testimony is often taking a huge risk, sometimes a physical risk, in making themselves publicly vulnerable. Paradoxically, by sharing their story publicly, they become more powerful, and the decision maker starts to look vulnerable and exposed through being "forced" to listen to the testimony.

In Walter Wink's reading of Matthew 5:38–40, Jesus asks his listeners to turn the other cheek and to give up both tunic and cloak: "You have heard that it was said, 'An eye for an eye and a tooth for a tooth.' But I say to you, Do not resist an evildoer [by force]. But if anyone strikes you on the right cheek, turn the other also; and if anyone wants to sue you and take your coat, give your cloak as well." In occupied first-century Galilee, if someone were to smack a social inferior on the cheek, the superior might use the back of the right hand. The back of the hand denotes superiority, and since the left hand is "unclean" due to its toileting association, the right hand is the only option. If the victim of the smack were to turn the other cheek, s/he would force the assailant into a dilemma. To smack the other cheek would entail either using the palm—denoting an equality that humiliates the attacker—or using the back of the left hand, thus breaking a taboo that would also humiliate the attacker. To turn the other cheek is not to give into violence, but to expose it.

Testimony that is well organised, personalised, and focused on a moral issue can turn a powerful decision maker from an opponent into an ally almost instantly. I witnessed this when teenage girls described their experience to persuade the Police and Crime Commissioner in Nottingham to make their region the first to recognise misogyny as a hate crime; and when a Black Bishop described his experience of police harassment to argue for changes to "stop and search." When my children see these brave activists stand on a stage and speak their experience to power, they are consequently seeing people they know, people whose courage they admire.

Finding Their Own Path

Martha is fourteen, and both her values and her way of doing politics are now being formed apart from me as much as with me. We now debate over what is and what is not worth the fight. Community Organising has shown my children that social activism is nothing without a clear set of values, a testable theory of change, and a willingness to risk failure. Their experience has been shaped by faith. It's not a faith they currently share, but nonetheless one that has formed their understanding of the world as it is and as it should be. A theory of change that builds a broad base of relational power to negotiate with positional power must, by definition, be diverse in every sense, including diverse in age. So it makes sense that broad-based Community Organising creates a public space where parents can introduce their children into social activism, shaped by their own faith or values, and give them experiences from which to learn and through which to grow.

Try It Out

- Make a list of all the places the young people in your care "belong." How can they start with these places to build relational power and create meaningful change?

- Have a relational meeting with the young people in your care. Share your stories, your anger, and your self-interest, and invite them to do the same.

- If you live in the UK, visit https://www.citizensuk.org to find out more about local organising, projects, and campaigns. Take a look at their schools organising work, for example, or register for training. If you live in the US, visit https://www.industrialareasfoundation.org.

13

Table Talk and Music Making

Don E. Saliers

How can we cultivate virtues of empathy, courage, generosity, justice, and humility at home in a time of distraction and multiple commitments? What family practices can we adopt to develop and sustain our sense of social and personal responsibility? In this chapter, I grapple with these questions retrospectively. My daughters are long grown-up. Three of them are social and political activists, and the fourth and youngest daughter was active with women's and minority rights' issues in Los Angeles before her unexpected death in 1999. While I now have quite some distance from the intensity of child-rearing years, I remember how in their emerging adolescent and adult lives each of our daughters was engaged beyond the home in a wide range of activities and relationships. We were constantly juggling different commitments and priorities. So how, I have been pondering, did we parent our four daughters to help form their capacities for social and political engagement as well as for creative individuality? What's more—and just as importantly—how did we as parents learn and grow in the process? How have our daughters taught us?

A central biblical question for my wife, Jane, and me was how best to trace in our family a deepening narrative of Jesus' way of being in the world. A version of a scripture passage from Philippians 4:8 over the lintel of our home was key in this deepening: "Finally beloved, whatever is true, whatever is honorable...if there is any excellence and if there is anything worthy of praise, think about these things." We encouraged our children (and they us) to live out such excellent and honorable things as well as ponder them. Experiencing and practicing these virtues in daily household life takes work. Part of such work lies in parents creating the conditions for their children to mature by making good choices, thinking of worthy things. We discovered that such wisdom is relational, for it is not justice but authority and even despotism if wisdom is one-sided, and we found that such wisdom requires practices, which likewise must be relational to be just, meaning in this case done by both parents and children, together.

Two such consistently shared activities or practices that Jane and I did regularly with our quartet of daughters were table talk and music making. I will describe these in a moment. First, let me set the scene to explain why we chose these two.

The older three girls were less than two years apart, while the fourth came along eight years later. They therefore had different developmental needs for us to take into account. We parents had both read Robert Coles's writings, especially *The Moral Lives of Children*.[86] But having both been raised as only children, the prospect of raising four concurrently was, in many ways, bewildering. So we took heart in the accounts in Coles's book of the moral resilience of children who lived in difficult circumstances. Added to that, the fact that both Jane's and my parents struggled with alcoholism alerted us to various forms of addiction. We brought that awareness to honest discussions at appropriate times. Perhaps that is why Coles's psychological and social insights were a significant background factor in our approach to our daughters' moral development.

Socially, our daughters grew up from the late 1960s to the early 1980s, a time of enormous societal change. Questions of racial, political, and personal identity were accelerating. The Vietnam War consumed the nation, and body counts were broadcast nightly on television. Images of burning cities, alongside marches and songs of protest, were playing daily in the media—and in the growing awareness of our young

[86]Robert Coles, *The Moral Lives of Children* (New York: Atlantic Monthly Press, 1986). Also, *The Spiritual Life of Children* (Boston: Houghton Mifflin, 1990).

daughters' minds. In that era, questions of gender and sexuality were also abroad in society and became increasingly important for the girls.

Raising four daughters during those tumultuous years in the US meant constantly facing questions that had not been part of Jane's and my childhood experiences. And with both of us eventually working full time (in university teaching and in the public library), we did our best. Yes, there were house rules, occasionally unevenly enforced. But what became most central to our daughters' formative moral and artistic development were conversations at the kitchen table, especially on Sundays, and our household's shared music practices.

Our aim, as privileged white parents, was to arrange conditions in our household that would prompt both moral and aesthetic imagination. Trusting good education in their schools was one thing; cultivating living together at home was another. Looking back, I think we did a lot of improvisation, and the language of music and art was something we could offer. But how to negotiate all these factors?

Table Talk

Initially, our Sunday meal conversations were often haphazard. But gradually they became a discipline, certainly a form of ritual practice. The main task was to set aside the time, but also allow for spontaneous and surprising moments, often after engagement in a local food pantry or community shelter or following an event in which the children participated. These events ranged from musicals, plays, and school festivals to more challenging and difficult happenings in the community (accidents, community change, projects such as a community garden, and neighborhood clean-ups, for example).

With time, Sunday meals around a common table became a kind of moral and religious forum for all of us. This was not so much a grand plan as it was an emergent discovery. From an early age each daughter began to take her place and have a voice at our weekly after-church meal conversations. Sometimes those conversations would begin with a question about what had happened at church. What did the preacher mean by saying such and such? Why did people in the Bible say and do what they did? Why was Jesus always getting into trouble? Why do the psalms talk about "enemies" and "sin" so much? No question was ruled out. As our daughters grew older, the theodicy question became more intense: Why is there so much suffering in the world? Mixed in with these heavy topics we shared a lot of ordinariness, some sad and much that was funny, even hilarious.

But this much was clear: Family conversations on Sundays after having shared the common custom of Sunday school and worship were different from the chaotic and sometimes scattered meals during the school week. The family gradually came to know that Sunday table talk was a regular place of free sharing. You might say that it was a key family ritual.

Yet though they typically happened on Sunday, often our family discussions had nothing to do with church or religion. They were often prompted by whatever was disturbing about events in their lives or in their relationships. What did someone experience as generating curiosity, or (often) questioning what the silence on a particular topic was about. Then there were those times when someone would actually report something good that had inspired them. One of them might say, "Did you see that movie, that vegetable garden?" On one occasion, our oldest daughter—after some silence one Sunday—broke into tears and told us that because two friends had cheated on a test the teacher had canceled the entire class's test results. Should she "rat" on them or not? She had lost a crucial good score on the test. "It's just not fair!" she complained, and her sisters chimed in, each sharing how unfair many things seemed to them. They expressed clear empathy with her plight. But this also led to a discussion of why both rules and punishment were to be taken seriously—at least that was the parental point of view. That particular episode stands out in my mind because the question of fairness was a recurring topic over many teen years. It later also encompassed how each daughter had to face troubling relationships with friends and rivals.

More domestic issues also got a hearing at that table. I recall the time I was so irritated with something one of them had done that I snapped, "That's it, you're grounded for a week, no talk back!" Hardly were the words out of my mouth than I knew I had overreacted. But there was great silence and considerable resentment that Saturday in the house. The following afternoon at Sunday table, the youngest finally broke the silence and said, "That's alright, Dad, we forgive you." She and her sisters had discerned that my unreasonable edict was, in part, a result of the pressure on both us parents. As I recall, tensions resulting from worries over unexpected expenses came up frequently (household expenses with four daughters in school was, for us at that particular time, always a hovering backstory). That word of forgiveness was a merciful moment. The children had understood more than we thought, and my own hasty judgment was revealed for what it was. This was part of what I think of as our education as parents.

Because we lived as a white family in an all-Black neighborhood for seven years, many of our conversations focused on our daughters' experiences at Helene Grant School and on the neighborhood encounters they had. Some of them were about perceived family cultural differences, and several were about how to deal with events with the presence and occasionally perceived threats with the Black Panthers down the street on Dixwell Avenue. "Why do white and Black people hate each other?" they'd ask in reaction to stories told. "This neighborhood is different; why?" Or, "We're friends, but there are funny reactions to us in school sometimes." These were actual topics of our conversations. Years later, each of our daughters would recall living in Florence Virtue Housing as sources of memory and struggle. This has been especially true of Emily's social justice work with the Indigo Girls and with indigenous peoples' causes. There are clear reasons why all four became involved in the local food pantry and hospital volunteering early on.

In such ways, over time, the Sunday kitchen table became a family space for moral and religious formation—for the development of our characters and the fostering of the virtues of empathy, courage, generosity, justice, and humility. Yet it was also a ritual place of mutual tension and encounter as each daughter progressed into adolescence. What I remember most is that, at those table meals, each daughter eventually gained her own voice. Of course, there were also the sullen times of "Our parents don't know anything!" Often this led to conversations with each, often initiated by their mother. There were times when I had to understand the limits of my ability to understand what they were going through. Thus, my learning as a father of four daughters was frequently filled with perplexity. I had to learn when *not* to be the "voice of wisdom." I also learned that when the tension and complexity of their lives was the most confusing, they desired both their mother's and their father's engagement. The practices of that

time and place, even when teenage resistance appeared successively—
and differently—in each of their lives, were both confessional and
formational. In short, we learned *from* and *with* one another. Practices
had become habits. By this time, we were aware of Murray Bowen and
Edwin Friedman and family systems theory—a theory that seeks to
understand human beings by exploring the interactions between the
members of a family and between the family and the context in which
they live. My wife and I used our experience of this version of "table
talk" (thank you, Martin Luther) to listen to one another more carefully.
I have, of course, discerned this in hindsight. One of our family sayings
developed, "We live forwards and understand backwards." Now, with
adult children raising their own, this seems a gift of practice. Romantic
nostalgia about their childhood they tend to avoid.

Music Making

The second touchstone practice of our parenting centered on music.
Ours was a house filled with instruments and song. From early on,
each daughter listened to tapes and records, sharing a lot together.
There was much silly singing, but also of expected participation. Some
car trips turned into choral improvisation sessions. I recall one such
occasion when they began a lovely four-part song from school choir.
Suddenly, Elizabeth began to sing her part a half-step higher. They
each hung on as long as possible to the other parts and finished with
gales of laughter. It was actually quite an accomplishment. No wonder
Elizabeth went on to study opera.

Each of them was eventually involved in school and church choirs.
We encouraged each daughter to pursue the particular kind of music
that she loved. Stories about car trips often found us doing narrative
singing in three and four parts. With some prodding, of course, each
girl took up an instrument—flute, cello, guitar, and piano. Looking
back now, I can see how each of them came to appreciate and
encourage one another; I think we were fortunate that they each
had their own musical domain—something made easier because we
tried to encourage highly individualized personalities. Elizabeth Jane
pursued classical vocal and instrumental interests, while her younger
sister, Carrie Christiana, found her deepest enjoyment and energy in
musical theatre and drama. The oldest, Jennifer, developed a life-long
interest in medieval music, eventually singing with the Atlanta Schola

Cantorum for many years, while the second-born daughter, Emily, became a well-known singer songwriter and political activist.

There was competition among them, but never in musical matters. How was that achieved? The best I can say is that we tried to create an atmosphere of mutual appreciation, supporting each in their various performances during their school years. Not that considerable scheduling wasn't a headache at times! There was a form of triage that we, as parents, were always negotiating. One of the most difficult issues concerned conflicting musical schedules in their schools. Sometimes we simply had to say, "We are going to your sister's concert, so we can't go to yours." Gradually, through times of family music making, each came to see that we parents gave each daughter equal interest and support. Our practice was encouraging them to listen and to appreciate one another's talent. This meant, of course, sharing in their failures and disappointments.

Obviously, one area that affected all four at one time or another was the problem of disciplined musical practice. It was especially heartening when we noticed how they praised (or consoled) one other's performances. This became part of shared music making at home. The pressure to "perform" was lessened because each eventually *wanted* to share what they were learning. This sharing I consider one of the most important aspect of each one's development.

We listened to and practiced many types of music. There was the shared singing of hymns and anthems (early on in children's choirs) in church. Eventually, three of the daughters sang with a touring Atlanta choral group. In this way a common repertoire of music developed among them. Because both of us parents sang, we took notice of the kinds of music each daughter began to prefer. The mix of classical orchestral and choral music alongside our mutual interest in jazz and various musicians (for example, early on, John Denver, Joni Mitchell, and popular bands that each daughter brought to our attention) was part of the soundtrack of the house. Looking back, it was singing together that was crucial. This was part of their emerging breadth of musical tastes. Cultivating joy in one another while listening or performing is central. This often led to discussions of what makes something "beautiful," but also to what they didn't like and why. In a way these family practices were like a slowly developing course in music appreciation.

But, you may be asking, how is learning to play an instrument or singing together connected with social justice? How did our family musical practices foster our sense of political and social responsibility? The links between music (beauty) and acting for justice (goodness) emerged early and became clearer over time. To come to love the music of another culture was to come to love people in that culture. To be challenged to appreciate the discipline and art of good music making sheds light on coming to appreciate the way others struggle with questions of moral goodness. This linkage is at the heart of what each of our daughters came to find important in their lives. Resistance to what is ugly and diminishing (such as misogyny and violence) is both an aesthetic and moral training. Observing this process in their growing up is one of the great lessons I received as a father. In a more day-to-day sense, learning an instrument or how to sing with others requires the development of the same virtues that are needed for social action: courage, collaborative spirit, humility, above all empathy. In our case, each daughter had a particular set of interests. Recall that our eldest came to love medieval music and thus for twenty-five years sang in Atlanta's Schola Cantorum presenting the "Play of Herod" each December for the whole community. Another daughter has had a long career as a touring and recording musician, while a third has enjoyed a recital career as a soprano and as a flute player. Our youngest was especially gifted in musical theatre. The obvious reward in all this was that music provided a form of individuation for each of them—a means through which they could develop their own unique personality. Their distinct musical gifts and habits were part of their process of becoming individuals, but individuals in relationship. The gift was also in their mutual support and encouragement. When our youngest daughter died, we felt a huge silence and discovered how deeply we missed her vitality and distinctive presence. Her sisters can speak of their concern for her, but also of the influence her own dedication to social causes had on them.

The idea of "becoming musical" with practice was, thus, clearly like "becoming honest" with practice. Musical and moral empathic imagination seemed to call out to one another in each of the daughters. It is analogous to developing a way of "hearing" and a way of "interpreting" patterns of sensibility. The qualities develop over time; the capacity to be oneself in relationship with others grows with practice.

Living Forwards, Understanding Backwards

Now that the older three are well into their adult lives, I have begun to understand what our parenting did well, and where we struggled along the way. The unexpected loss of the youngest daughter, and the death of their mother, Jane, a decade later has given me a way of seeing patterns in parenting in a more complex, poignant tonality. I have come to notice the interplay of intimacy and mutual accountability, and the necessity of "letting be" at every stage of the parenting process. Mortality has a way of framing and focusing the larger pattern of how virtues and dispositions are formed and expressed over time.

There was (and is), of course, far more to family life than the kitchen table and the music; and many of you may not count music among one of your particular passions. You may have other creative and artistic interests—from drama and dance to crafting, painting, or interior design to woodworking or cooking. What I am talking about here is engaging in any kind of practice of creativity together that fosters our moral and aesthetic sensibilities and skills simultaneously. Perhaps the process underlying all of family life was more akin to Mary Oliver's poetic mantra, "Pay attention."[87] This is not an easy discipline. We, like all parents, needed time and space for ourselves. So impatience with adolescence—each in her own time—had its own rhythm. There was in my experience always the rhythm of distraction and return. The return to empathy and love so often occurred when each daughter in turn faced decisions and crises of her own. To hold and to rediscover how precious and interesting their lives were always drew us back, especially in light of our separate careers outside the home. Openness to learning from them was our mutual covenant. Now, when my daughters have begun to care for me in explicit and implicit ways, I have become the object of their attention in ways that recapitulate the care that our own parenting required. I have learned that respect and mutuality are not givens but are ongoing practices. Now, in the later stage of my life, I can only wonder at what that quartet (present and absent) have given back. This is the slowly disclosed joy and poignancy of parenting.

I mentioned earlier that a critical dimension of my backstory is the demand of raising all daughters in a society like ours. That context—

---

[87]"Paying attention" is a constant theme in her poetry. See Mary Oliver, "Praying," in *Devotion* (New York: Penguin Random House, 2017), 131.

rife with questions of sexual identity, empowerment, and social commitments—pushed me to learn how to be appropriately and realistically protective and encouraging of my daughters' freedom as women in this culture. This became a constant theme of self-reflection, both for me as a parent and for them in their maturing relationships. Each daughter is deeply committed to justice and peace issues, and each is socially active in her own way—from engaging in community food banks to political protesting to working with indigenous peoples. That they are flourishing and they have embraced activism at each stage tells me that "coming to maturity" is a mysterious process. So much depends on consistent practices and a steady environment of mutual attentiveness. So much depends on a kitchen table and a lot of singing and music making together. They also take great interest in one another's different community and social justice work, a pattern established in those many years of Sunday kitchen table talks and common musical pursuits. Over years they learned to take delight in one another's accomplishments. At the same time, we came to appreciate the times of struggle and difficulty. In the words of one Emily's songs, we had learned how to live "Closer to Fine."[88] And we had done so together.

Try It Out

- Choose one weekly mealtime—the same each week—at which you can sit down to eat together as a family and have table talk. A regular rhythm is important. Use this time to have intentional conversations about what is going on for your children, to listen carefully to one another, and to grapple together with the observations or questions they have.

- Hold "conversation" meals with neighboring families raising teens—preferably allowing the younger people to cook or plan the meal—with conversation around whatever is on their minds.

- Urge your local community to sponsor front porch music sharing. This local festival could feature a wide age range of children along with adult bands and soloists.

---

[88]Indigo Girls, "Closer to Fine," track 1 on *Indigo Girls,* Epic Records, 1989, CD.

- Explore a wide variety of creative outlets and follow the distinct creative interests of your family: dance, drama, painting, drumming, woodworking. Think together about the ways each creative pursuit takes courage and fosters empathetic practices (listening to others, supporting others, seeing connections).

- Encourage your children or grandchildren to interview local artists on what shaped their music, especially on questions of practice and musical discipline, and why they call certain music "good."

Afterword

In this book, we have invited you to try out practices that we find to be practical, meaningful, and joyful. The variety here reflects our different stages of life, family situations, and challenges we experience as parents and activists. We invite you to sing subversive lullabies to your babies, talk about kindness with your toddlers, and plant edible gardens with your young ones. We invite you to pray with your kids, to make music together, to make art and practice meditation. We invite you to conduct relational meetings and focus groups with children, to listen to what they value, wonder about, mourn, desire, and imagine. We also invite you to pause, to slow down, to wait, to sit with the interruption. And we invite you to protest together, to pack up essential items to give to others, and to organize for change together.

We offer these not as items to add to your overflowing to-do lists. Rather, we offer them as practices for you to consider integrating into your lives. Practices are more than tasks that you need to complete. Practices are not just activities we *do*; they shape who we *are* and who we are *becoming*. They are the embodiment of our convictions; they help our lives to reflect the beliefs we hold; they help us to live into our commitments; they are formative.

We hope that these practices are helpful to you in and of themselves and as ideas that spark your own imagination and creativity. We hope that they are generative—that they open up possibilities for you and for your family, help you to think in fresh ways about activities that you already do and how you might do them with greater intention. Unlike an item on the to-do list that gets crossed off when completed, practices generate something new. They lead to other things. They open up space in our lives for other possibilities. They give us energy and sustenance to grow and to imagine and to build.

While not everything on our to-do lists can or should be developed into a practice (a lot of it just has to get done!), there might be items on your list that you could reframe with greater intention. And, in a broader sense, there might be activities in the regular rhythm of family life that you could do with greater purpose and care, such that they take on the quality of a formational practice for you and for your family.

We also hope that the voices collected here offer some encouragement for you. Whether you take up a particular practice or not, let yourself be encouraged by the thought that someone somewhere is doing that good thing. People all over are parenting for a better world. We are trying in our own ways to make this beautiful planet a more just place where our children and our children's children will flourish. Take heart knowing you are not alone and that every little action you take matters. God is present always and everywhere doing a new thing, taking our small everyday offerings and weaving them into a better world for all.

Contributors

Brian Brock is Professor of Moral and Practical Theology at the University of Aberdeen. He lives in Aberdeen, UK, and has three children.

Anton Flores-Maisonet is Founding Director of Casa Alterna. He lives in Decatur, Georgia, USA, and has experienced parenting through natural birth, adoption, and fostering.

Leah Gunning Francis is Vice President for Academic Affairs and Dean of the Faculty at Christian Theological Seminary. She lives in Indianapolis, Indiana, USA and has two children.

Keith Hebden is a Community Organiser with Citizens UK. He lives in Oxford, UK, and has two children.

HyeRan Kim-Cragg is Timothy Eaton Memorial Church Professor of Preaching at Emmanuel College of Victoria University in the University of Toronto. She lives in Toronto, Ontario, Canada, and has two children.

Luke Larner is a Church of England priest, currently serving as Assistant Curate at St. Paul's Church, Bedford. He lives in Bedford, UK, and has one child.

Carlton Mackey is the creator of Black Men Smile® and Director of the Ethics & the Arts Program at the Emory University Center for Ethics. He lives in Atlanta, Georgia, USA, and has one child.

Ellen Ott Marshall is Professor of Christian Ethics & Conflict Transformation at Candler School of Theology, Emory University. She lives in Atlanta, Georgia, USA, and has three children.

Chine McDonald is Director of Theos. She lives in London, UK, and has one child and another on the way.

Melissa Pagán is Associate Professor and Director of Graduate Religious Studies at Mount Saint Mary's University. She lives in Los Angeles, California, USA, and has three children.

Ingrid C. Arneson Rasmussen is Lead Pastor of Holy Trinity Lutheran Church in Minneapolis. She lives in Minneapolis, Minnesota, USA, and has two children.

Don E. Saliers is Wm. R. Cannon Distinguished Professor of Theology and Worship, Emeritus, and Theologian-in-Residence at Candler School of Theology, Emory University. He lives in Atlanta, Georgia, USA, and has four children.

Susanna Snyder is Academic Dean and Lecturer in Theology and Ethics at Ripon College, Cuddesdon. She lives in Oxford, UK, and has two children.